# Sixpence for the Wind

*The fishing fleet in Anstruther harbour, c.1895.*
Courtesy of Central Library, Dundee.

# Sixpence for the Wind

## A Knot of Nautical Folklore

Malcolm Archibald

With pen and ink drawings by Sarah Jane Adams

Whittles Publishing

Typeset by
**Whittles Publishing Services**

Published by
**Whittles Publishing**,
Roseleigh House,
Latheronwheel,
Caithness, KW5 6DW,
Scotland, UK



ISBN 1-870325-57-5

Printed by J.W.Arrowsmith Ltd., Bristol

# Contents

*A whaling ship and small paddle steamer, Dundee.*
Courtesy of Central Library, Dundee.

*for Cathy*

# Introduction

The seachests of before-the-mast mariners were frequently filled with personal treasures. A shell from the Seychelles, a poncho from Peru, the horn of a narwhal: each one priceless with memories, each one the key to a host of stories.

To open Davy Jones's Locker is to glimpse something of the sea's abundance. Each reef, each rock, each cove has a tale, and if the sea soon conceals the furrow of a keel, then the tongue and pen of man must record what remains. For this is our heritage. The high seas are international. They must remain so, for they are the only truly free space in the world.

Not all sea lore can be categorised, and in that shines the individuality of the seaman.

Where else is left termed port and right starboard? Where else is the front the bow, the back the stern? Where is a wall called a bulkhead, a floor a deck and a ladder a companionway? And only at sea is the passage of time marked by a bell. Mystical things these bells, and quite commonly found in the aftermath of a wreck. That was the case when HMS *Lutine* sailed from Yarmouth in October 1799. She had bullion on board, but ran aground on a Zuider Zee sandbank. The only survivor died soon after, and it was not until 1858 that some £50,000 was salvaged, together with the ship's rudder and bell.

While the rudder was refashioned into the chair for the Chairman of Lloyds, the bell was hung in the same office and rings once for every reported wreck, twice for every overdue ship.

Ships' bells signal the passage of time aboard. The day is divided into six watches of four hours each, except for the dog-watches which run from four bells until six pm and from six until eight pm. The bell rings to mark each half hour of every watch; one bell in the first dog watch would be four-thirty, two bells would be five o'clock.

According to sealore, five bells in the dog-watches was to signal the start of the 1797 mutiny. When the officers heard of this, they had one bell struck instead, and ever since then one bell has been struck at 6:30 pm.

Before the invention of the compass, ships used a lodestone to point north. For that reason mediaeval pilots were known as lodesmen. Seamen were not permitted to eat garlic or onions, as both these were detrimental to the effects of a lodestone – according to legend.

Even more unlucky than eating garlic was killing the stormy petrel. This little bird was known to seamen as Mother Carey's Chicken and at one time was believed to contain the soul of a drowned seaman.

The belief that the albatross was similarly protected seems to be a myth, as many seamen used pipe stems made from an albatross wing, and a tobacco pouch from the webbed foot of the same bird was common. However, in 1908 the brassbounders of the barque *Inverness* hooked and caught an albatross – and shortly after, the helmsman was killed.

Perhaps the albatross legend began with the voyage of Captain George Shelvocke. In September 1719 his ship was followed round the Horn by a black albatross, which seemed to attract storms. For days the bird remained with them and the weather did not improve until it was shot by Hatley, the second captain.

To many seamen the albatross was the Cape Sheep as it was so common around the Cape of Good Hope.

Also near the Cape, in a shady square overlooking the yacht basin at Simonstown, there is a statue to a seadog. This is Just Nuisance, once an Able Seaman in the Royal Navy. Originally Just Nuisance belonged to the manager of the United Services Institute but when he took to accompanying seamen on the Capetown train the Railway authorities complained. So the Navy signed Just Nuisance.

With his trade given as 'Bonecrusher', his religion as either 'scrounger' or 'canine divinity league: anti vivisectional' and his character as 'very good', Just Nuisance became a land based seadog. He drank at the seamen's pubs, guided those who had imbibed too freely back to the naval base and treated ordinary seamen as his equal. Petty Officers he could tolerate, but officers he just ignored.

On one occasion he saved the life of a seaman who lay stabbed and bleeding in an alley. Just Nuisance barked and howled until help arrived, but he was seriously hurt while jumping from a bus in January 1944. Two hundred seamen stood, heads bared in his honour as the White Ensign, last post and a firing party signalled the burial of a dog and the birth of some unique sea lore.

If seagoing animals added to the lore of the Navy, it was not unknown for less than scrupulous seamen to exploit this. When two matelots attempted to leave the dockyard at Chatham while carrying a large wicker basket, the dockyard police stepped in to stop them. 'What's in the basket lads?' Seamen being what they were, thoughts of smuggled rum were in the policeman's head.

'The ship's cat,' one of the seamen explained. 'The ship's in for a refit and we're taking him home to be safe.'

The police considered for a moment and decided that they did not believe the story. They demanded to see inside. A massive ginger cat, all claws and fur and fury, tore itself from the basket and back into the dockyard. Cursing openly, the seamen pursued their pet and, twenty minutes later returned to the dockyard gates. This time the police did not demand to see inside the basket.

Perhaps they should have, for inside were thousands of duty-free cigarettes. The matelots found a comfortable pub and toasted the ginger cat they had abducted to act as cover.

Unfortunately for the Navy, stricter laws on rabies forced their sea-pets ashore although they had a longer cruise in the East. Ben of H.M.S. *Wasperton* of the Hong Kong Patrol Craft Squadron is reputed to be the last Royal Naval dog. Or perhaps just the last *known* Royal Naval dog? There may be more to add to this particular fund of lore.

Lore too, sits on the shoulders of John Masefield, the poet whose 'Sea Fever' is both a favourite and a classic among seafaring men, although Masefield barely served his apprenticeship before the mast.

With less literary talent but more sea blood was the son of Captain Louis Casabiance, who refused to leave his father's side aboard *L'Orient*. The Battle of the Nile was in progress and both died.

*The boy stood on the burning deck*
*Whence all but he had fled*
*The flame that lit the battle's wreck*
*Shone round him o'er the dead.*

Other forgotten seamen include the famous Sam Colt. As a teenager Colt was in the brig *Carlo* bound from Connecticut to India, and he watched the helmsman steer the ship. The mechanism of the wheel fascinated him; whichever way the wheel turned, each spoke fitted exactly into line with a securing clutch.

From that, Colt carved out a model for the world's first revolving pistol.

Davy Jones has many such things in his locker.

# 1 Brass Monkeys and Swinging Cats

It's an expression we've all heard at one time or other, and thought nothing of. A raw morning in winter; one of those drab days when the northeast wind carries more than a hint of snow and people huddle deep into the warmth of an overcoat. There is a stamping of feet and much glowering at the pale grey sky until somebody, possibly hoping to be humorous, uses the old statement:

'It's cold enough to freeze the balls off a brass monkey.'

A man might grunt in agreement, others would say nothing as the vaguely obscene words drift into forgetfulness. But perhaps the old ghost of a long gone seafarer would stir as the memory of bitter frost that penetrated the salt hazed shroud of time.

To a naval man of two centuries ago there was deep meaning in that phrase.

It was wartime, and Britain was fighting for her existence. The armies of Napoleon were clustered on the coast of France, waiting their chance to clamber into the invasion barges and cross the Channel. If they had landed, there would have been only the gaudy militia to repel them, backed by a few thousand hard used redcoats. But first they had to land, and to do that they had to defeat the Royal Navy.

If the British army was minuscule and the militia amateur, the Navy was the epitome of professionalism. Week after week, year after year, the wooden ships with wind-battered sails patrolled the seas. In the heat of the tropics where the pitch bubbled between the holystoned planking of the deck; in the chops and unpredictable squalls of the North sea, and in the sub-zero chill of the Arctic where the whalers were convoyed home with their cargoes of whale bone and oil.

Even in those northern latitudes the Navy had to be prepared for action, for Bonaparte's privateers were daring and could cut out a blubber ship between the fading of the Pole Star and the ice blink of dawn. The iron cannonballs were ready in the racks, or monkeys as they were known, and if the cold made the balls contract, it had the same effect on the iron monkeys so no harm would result. But not on the flagship. Here, where the Commodore or Admiral hid the cares of responsibility behind the mask of comfort, the monkeys were of brass, which does not contract with the cold. So, every so often on the coldest of days, the iron balls would shrink enough to slip through the retaining bars of their monkey. On these days it was truly cold enough to freeze the balls off a brass monkey.

The heritage of language is a fascinating subject, and one that helps unravel the complicated strands that make up the history of any people. Words and phrases that occur every day have often evolved from undreamed-of sources, and the sea has provided more than its share. And that is as it should be, given the importance of seafaring to the islands of Britain.

At the time of the Flood, Noah floated his Ark and cruised the high seas, secure in the knowledge that, as his family alone had been chosen, there would be no other craft on the water. He was wrong; according to Hebridean folklore, MacNeil of Barra had his own boat.

If that story is perhaps apocryphal, it does illustrate the extent of maritime folklore in these islands.

Many expressions have become part of everyday land language; others have slipped into obscurity after a period of hard usage. One of these is the phrase 'son of a gun' which enjoyed a century or more of use as an insult, before retreating in the face of sterner language, although it seems to have sporadic outings in America. Again it dates back to the old sailing days and rips aside a veil concealing the women who shared this harsh life with their men.

Many of these were wives, others were sweethearts and inevitably some became mothers while on board. This would be a frantic experience, with only coarse screens of canvas for privacy and the midships cannon for support. The resulting children were written into the ship's books under the name of the mother and, where known, the father. If the father was not known, the child became the 'son of a gun'. In land language, illegitimate.

Another, now less well used, phrase is 'cut and run'. This is a very old saying that originated in times of trouble. Before the days of chains and steel hawsers, the anchor cable of any ship was made of hemp.

In 1588 the Spanish Armada lay at anchor off Calais when the English sent in their fireships. That created panic. The Spanish were experienced mariners who had opened up the maritime world, but fire at sea was a terrible thing. Ordering the cables cut, the Spaniards ran before the wind. One hundred and fifty anchors were sunk in the sands of Calais and if no Spanish ships were lost to the English 'Devil Ships', the fleet was scattered and began the long, destructive retreat round Britain.

On land, to cut and run meant to leave some enterprise and disappear at speed. Frequently there was no great honour in this procedure.

There are many other less obvious terms borrowed from the sea. The simple phrase 'I hail from' as in 'I hail from Dundee' comes from hailing a ship, while 'flotsam and jetsam', now meaning anything not wanted, had a very nautical beginning.

Flotsam meant anything found floating on the sea and jetsam, from the French jeter, to throw out, meant anything thrown overboard. In time this evolved into any wreckage that drifted ashore.

Sometimes not everything that came ashore was legal. The old smuggling trade provided at least a couple of everyday terms. Free trade is today used to denote a lack of tariff barriers although originally it meant the practice of smuggling, avoiding the customs. These free traders were highly organised, with darkened luggers coming to a pre-arranged rendezvous to be met by fishing boats which 'ran' the illicit cargo to the shore. Here it could be received by a hundred or more packhorses that carried the goods inland.

Of course all this would be pointless if the Excisemen 'caught wind' – another nautical term – of the operation. So the smugglers posted sentries to watch for the activities of the Excise. If it was safe the signal was given:

'The coast is clear' – and the cargo came ashore.

Some words are so commonplace that it seems almost discourteous to delve into their origins. 'Tidy' is one of these; to be tidy is to be neat, to keep things in good order. This word is from the Old English for the tide – as orderly and regular as the tide itself.

Almost opposite in meaning is 'junk' which has come to represent general rubbish. The original meaning was old or condemned rope or cord, this possibly being derived from the Latin 'juncus', a type of rush used in cord manufacture.

Then there are words which refer to articles of clothing. The most obviously nautical is 'reefer'; a short, double-breasted coat or jacket that was at one time exclusive to seamen and now is fairly common on land. 'Blazer' is another, although the origin for that word is based more on folklore than hard fact.

Back in the early 19th century there was no fixed uniform for the hands on board Naval ships and their captain dressed them as he thought appropriate. Obviously the more wealthy the captain, the more capable he was of maintaining a dress code, and while most captains used the cheapest of materials doled out from the slop chest, others were more particular.

The captain of HMS *Blazer* dressed his ship's company in jerseys of bright red and white stripes so in time any brightly striped jacket became a 'blazer'.

For many years, only seamen wore trousers while landsmen wore breeches, although neither the name nor the article began life at sea. This had a practical reason, for men scrubbing or washing down the deck of a heeling ship needed to roll up the legs of their trousers, which could not be done in the far tighter-fitting breeches.

Many nautical expressions seem to have kept a similar meaning, if in a more prosaic manner, after being transferred to the land. 'Bale out' for instance, which means to empty unwanted water out of a boat. This smacks of adventure and long horizons. On land it merely means to give a hand, and frequently implies the lending of money.

This would happen if somebody was 'hard up' or broke. At sea if a ship had to turn away from the wind because of heavy weather, the helm was put 'hard up' to windward in order to alter course. A hard up man had to 'weather the storm' of his poverty. He would then have a choice. He could hide his penury or 'sail under false colours' by pretending he was something he was not, as was done by those fighting ships that wished to take another vessel unawares; or he could save as best he could and 'keep on course' for better days. When these days arrived he would be on an 'even keel.'

A ship on an even keel was cruising along nicely, not heeling with the pressure of wind, while on land the words mean everything is all right; life, or a situation, is in balance.

The phrase 'square meal' is another nautical adaptation, now meaning a meal of satisfying proportions, but in the old Navy meaning food served on the square wooden plates of shipboard life.

Frequently people are 'taken aback' by a surprising event, and at sea it could certainly be a surprise, for that meant the wind had changed direction and pressed the sails against the mast. This would result in a sudden and probably unwelcome halt to the ship's progress and trouble for the helmsman. If this happened the captain might well be at 'loggerheads' with the officer on watch, and stern language would result. The original loggerhead was an iron ball with a handle attached. This was heated in the galley fire, and used to keep pitch hot.

If a person was 'well set up' he was wealthy or well dressed, while a well set up ship was one with splendidly appointed rigging. Such a person could 'cut a fine feather', which at sea refers to the feather or bow wave of an advancing vessel.

If 'clear the decks' is an obvious expression meaning to get rid of anything that is non-essential, and 'in the Doldrums' equally clearly refers to those drowsy, listless areas of light winds in the tropics, why should somebody say, 'If ...does not ...I'll eat my hat?'

This harks back to the days before it became acceptable for men to eat sweets, and chewing gum was not the widespread habit it has now become. On board ship, men chewed a wad of tobacco which, when removed from the mouth, was stored under their hat. With neither pockets nor privacy this made sense. In time the tobacco juice would soak into the lining and permeate the fabric of the hat, so 'eat my hat' was perhaps not such a strange expression.

'Blood is thicker than water' is relatively modern, and was actually a statement made by Commodore Josiah Tattnall of the US Navy. It was June 1859 and the

Royal Navy was trying to force its way past the Taku Forts in the Chinese War. For once the Navy was having the worst of it and the gunboat *Plover* had lost most of her crew. Nine out of forty were left, still fighting furiously.

The Americans were neutral in this war, but Tattnall's launch helped rescue some of the British wounded. Ignoring diplomatic niceties, some of the American seamen also helped the gun crew of the *Plover*. When Tattnall had to report the matter to Washington he defended his men, 'Blood' he wrote, 'is thicker than water.'

'No room to swing a cat' recalls a less pleasant memory. The image of a squealing feline being swung by the tail is totally inaccurate, for the cat in question had nine tails and was used for punishment. Apparently the number nine, significant as a 'trinity of trinities', was thought to increase the penitence of the offender.

Equally nasty was the 17th century phrase of kid nabbing, now become kidnapping. This was a reprehensible crime when a youngster was nabbed, or grabbed, and sold to an unscrupulous ship's captain. In turn the captain transported the child – or a cargo of such children – to the American colonies to be sold on the plantations.

The slave trade was not confined to Africa.

There are many other phrases; to be 'first rate', a warship had to boast at least 98 guns, while a ship beating along a coast was sailing 'off and on'. Waves crashing onto a deck and pouring from stem to stern were performing a 'clean sweep'; the expression 'pipe down', meaning to make less noise came from the bosun's call of 'hands turn in.'

And then there is the well known 'posh.' This came from a period both later and more luxurious than the majority of nautical expressions. The days of the great P & O Liners when the bright young things mingled with the colonial administrators on their way to some backwater of India or Africa.

Those who could afford it chose a cabin on the port side, the side away from the sun, on the outward voyage, and a cabin on the starboard, again the shady, side on the return. Port Out, Starboard Home – Posh.

But the last phrase mentioned should be 'the bitter end'. Not the final twist of bad fortune, or the person who holds out through all the vagaries of fate, but the last part of the cable which is fastened to the bitts to prevent it falling overboard.

That was the bitter end.

# The Non-existent

Many miles to the east of China there is a huge chasm into which all the waters of the world plunge. This is the Kuei-Hui and above this were five marvellous islands, each populated by the Immortals, who ate the plants of immortality. These islands were fastened to large tortoises but when a giant came to fish for these animals, two of the islands floated free and eventually sank.

That left three islands and many expeditions were sent to locate them. They all failed. Explorer after explorer returned with tales of floating islands, or of islands that inverted themselves, or of islands that sank beneath the surface of the sea.

Much of this may be apocryphal; it is unlikely that there were ever islands full of immortals, but the mirage of a floating island, or of an inverted island, can sometimes be seen.

With this mixture of folklore, myth and fantasy, the Chinese interest in their maritime surroundings appears no different to that of other nations.

This searching for, and often sighting, the non-existent, has continued into very recent times and, no doubt, continues today. Although we no longer search for unknown islands, who is to say that some of the things we do seek will not be scoffed at by future generations with more knowledge than we possess?

There was Juan Ponce de Leoa, who searched for the famed Fountain of Youth in 1513. Instead he found Florida, now a haven for tourists.

There was the Arctic explorer John Ross who reported his progress barred by a range of mountains. Perhaps they appeared plain to him, but they did not exist. For a few years Croker's Mountains appeared on the maps, until a later expedition sailed right through their theoretical position.

Then there was Crocker Land. This was seen on the 24th June 1906 by the American Arctic explorer Robert E. Peary. A few days later Crocker Land was seen again and Peary wrote:

> *My heart leaped the intervening miles of ice as I looked longingly at this land, and in fancy I trod its shores, and climbed its summits.*

Eight years later an expedition found no trace of the place and all references to Crocker Land were scrubbed off the map.

There's no shame in a seaman being deceived by nature's practical jokes. Even James Cook, one of the most skilled navigators who ever sailed, was caught out. There is an island in Halifax Bay, Queensland that Cook named Magnetic Island because of its supposed effects on his compass. Subsequently, other seamen failed to confirm this.

James Cook was one of the many navigators sent to ascertain the location of a southern continent, Terra Australis Incognito. There is an early example of political correctness in the naming of Cook's ships. Originally they were to be *Drake* and *Raleigh* but this was altered to *Discovery* and *Resolution* in case the original names offended the Spanish.

Scientific opinion of the 18th century believed that there must be a landmass in the southern hemisphere to balance the bulk of Eurasia in the north. To discover this place, various governments recruited scientists and explorers, packed them into ships and sent them south.

Their orders were simple: find the Great South Land. It must be there; Ptolemy the ancient scholar and the 10th century Flemish geographer Abraham Ortelius both said that it was. As they had neither proof nor location, it was up to the harassed Naval commanders to find land.

In 1722 the Dutchman Jacob Roggeveen commanded and funded a fleet to locate this continent. Instead he discovered Easter Island. Very romantic, but not the continent he'd hoped for.

This was perhaps not the first European sighting of Easter Island for back in 1683 the buccaneer Edward Davis had noted 'a small, sandy island' and had 'heard a great noise like that of the sea beating apon the shore right ahead of the ship'.

Davis was captain of the aptly named *Bachelor 's Delight* which had been off the coast of West Africa. At that time John Cook had been in command; he exchanged his own vessel for sixty young African girls, who he took with him. Cook died off the Mexican coast and Davis took command.

Possibly more intriguing was another sighting by Davis when he saw 'a range of high land which we took to be an island'. This latter sighting became known as Davis's Land. It was this high land which encouraged Roggeveen to hunt for the Southern Continent.

After Roggeveen came the Frenchman Yves Joseph de Kerguelen-Tremarel. In 1772 he saw, dimly through the fog, the small island group which now bears the name Kerguelen. Returning next year, Kerguelen explored more fully, and was disappointed to find no continent.

Samuel Wallis was next. During a two-year circumnavigation he discovered the delights of Tahiti, the Wallis Islands and little else. Folklore says that some of his seamen returned with tattoos which furthered, or even began, the trend for body decoration in mariners.

Then came James Cook of Yorkshire, the epitome of maritime explorers. Cook learned his trade in the North Sea coasters, one of the hardest apprenticeships known to man. Bare feet, bare deck, barely any food and a school for superb seamen. Even the captains here were known as 'bears' by other seamen, for they were mainly illiterate, coarse and very hardy.

Cook honed his skills in the Navy and spent eight years surveying Newfoundland and St. Lawrence. Then came the Pacific. Cook spent three voyages and the best part of eleven years unlocking the secrets of the Pacific. By the time he was killed at Karakoka Bay in Hawaii there was little left to discover.

The coasts of Eastern Australia, New Zealand and part of Antarctica had been surveyed. An attempt to passage between Asia and North America had been found impractical. Limits had now been set on the world and most of the blanks lay on the interiors.

With Cook we have the last great maritime explorer. But, ironically, much of this information was already known.

The Dutchman Abel Tasman had preceded Cook by over a century. Tasman had discovered Tasmania and named it Van Diemen's Land after Antony Van Diemen the governor general of Batavia who had sent him out. He also discovered New Zealand, Tonga and Fiji and had circumnavigated Australia without actually seeing it.

If the Dutch had followed up Tasman's explorations, they could have been first to colonise Australia, with who knows what consequences. But as Columbus had offered his services to Henry VII of England and had been rejected, that probably evens things out.

Imagine Henry VIII or Elizabeth Tudor with the riches of the New World at their disposal – now that would be to dream of the non-existent.

Towards the opposite pole there was another object that fascinated generations of seamen, and possibly even more armchair-bound theorists. This was the hope of a passage north of the American landmass. To the very rational mind there should exist such a passage to counterbalance Drake Passage or the Strait of Magellan in the south.

By the 16th century Spain controlled the southern route so the remaining European maritime nations hoped to reach the east by sailing north of America. It was a desperate, bold theory and hundreds of men were to die proving it false.

John Cabot took five ships to find Cipango – Japan – by this route. Only one vessel returned. Henry VIII sent out two ships; one was lost in an Atlantic storm, the other touched on land where her master found the footprints of a bear.

Jacques Cartier tried, and cruised up the St Lawrence to find the sites of both Quebec and Montreal. But not the Orient.

Men looked further north and during three centuries of courageous failure, of agonisingly creeping cartography, they filled in the tortuous map of Arctic Canada. The names of captains who were frustrated by the impossible are like sea legends, frost rimmed and bitter.

Frobisher sailed this way, and Henry Hudson who was set adrift in the huge bay that bears his name. He left a widow, but she did not weep long before setting off for the east to make her fortune in Ahmedabad.

John Davies tried and is remembered by Davis Strait. He died at the sword edge of Japanese pirates east of Singapore.

In May 1612 the Welshman Thomas Button was sent to the north and although he failed to return with the '...good news of a Passage' that was hoped for, he did discover that there was no way west from Hudson Bay. After him came the pilot William Baffin of London, with the hopeful instruction to bring back a native of Japan. He reached latitude 77°45´N but could not find a way through the ice. 'Hope of passage' he reported, 'could be none.' Like Davis, he died in the East, shot at the siege of Ormuz.

Luke Foxe tried, and had as much trouble with his compass as had Cook at Magnetic Island. Deep in the Arctic he met the Welshman Captain James and the two captains argued.

In June 1719 James Knight tried, and died. Christopher Middleton tried, found a hopeful inlet in Hudson Bay and reported that most of his press-ganged seamen were rogues. Probably they had equally hard things to say about the captain who had them pressed.

Vitus Bering had no more success from the Asian side. Perhaps the fact that he searched for the mythical land of Gamaland hindered his exploration. He did find Alaska but died in a shipwreck on Bering Island.

Commander John Byron was sent to discover both the North West Passage and the Great South Land in a single sweeping voyage. He failed in both objectives.

Captain Constantine Phipps tried to sail over the North Pole to Asia. He failed too, not surprisingly.

Attempts by land were interesting. Hearne and Alexander Mackenzie both had success but in so doing more or less proved there was no sea passage.

Not convinced or too stubborn to give up, governments and industrialists financed more explorers, more expeditions. Ross, who was thwarted by Croker's Mountains; William Parry, who sailed hundreds of icy miles into Lancaster Sound until the frozen sea turned him back, and John Franklin, who disappeared in the north.

John Ross tried again and survived miraculously. His nephew James Clark Ross found the magnetic North Pole. Robert McClure and Francis McClintock made their mark and, finally, Roald Amunsden tried in 1903.

He succeeded.

By then it was far too late. The passage, what there was of it, was uneconomic, virtually unnavigable and useless for anything but personal prestige. But as an enduring background to courage, skill and determination, the Northwest Passage has few equals.

Unlike the search for Atlantis.

Luckily this has been more a literary and library search than one of actual physical involvement, for there is no such place. Never was, really, at least not in the manner or in the area that pseudoscholars, ancient philosophers and various dreamers would hope.

The legend began when an Athenian named Solon sailed to Egypt. Here he heard about an island kingdom that had vanished into the sea in a single day. The story came down through word of mouth to Plato, and the name Atlantis somehow became attached. Plato's description pointed to a huge island in the west, maybe in the Atlantic. Yet the Egyptians were land based, their ships little more than riverboats and they certainly knew less of the western seas than did the Greeks. And prior to Solon's visit, the Greeks knew nothing of Atlantis.

The Phoenicians might have. Folklore claims that they knew of some mysterious continent, but that could have been Britain, or even Spain.

Because many people shared the legend, there may be some truth. The Greeks called the place Atlantis; the Phoenicians Antila; the Egyptians Aneti; the Berbers Atalaintika; all Mediterranean people, and all seemed to think that this place was in the Atlantic.

It was not. Although Atlantis was marked on maps until the mid $19^{th}$ century, geological surveys have quashed this location.

But there is a possibility that Atlantis was in fact the island of Thera in the Cyclades. In about 1500 BC this was the scene of a massive volcanic explosion which tore the centre from the island. This was no continent, but the result of this volcanic activity would have been very destructive to nearby Crete. Possibly bad enough to damage the Minoan civilisation there.

Or perhaps the entire story was just that; a story.

# 3 Sea Monsters

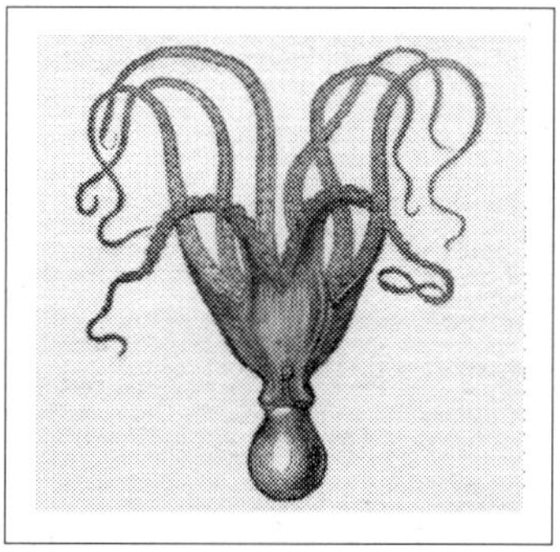

*'Yonder is the sea, great and wide,*
*which teems with things innumerable,*
*living things both small and great.*
*There go the ships,*
*And Leviathan which thou didst*
*form to sport in it.'*

Psalm 104; verses 25 and 26

There can be few people in the western world who have not heard of the Loch Ness Monster, or of the similar beasts which appear in widely scattered locations. The creature of Saddle Lake in Canada; the creature seen in Zegryzynski Lake in Poland; the unknown large shape in Lake Hanan, China or the long-necked creature which disturbed Lake Labinkir in Siberia. All have been sighted in the past couple of centuries.

All these creatures have two things in common; they have never been proved to exist, and they are in enclosed bodies of water.

Compared to these entrapped places, the sea is immense; a vast, still only partially-explored totality, teeming with life. All through the history of man's maritime adventure, there have been reports of meetings with unknown sea creatures, of sea monsters.

One of the best recorded is in the Bible, when the unlucky Jonah was tossed overboard to be immediately swallowed by a great fish. Whatever this creature was, and speculation has ranged from a whale to a hippopotamus, it consumed Jonah whole and kept him inside, unharmed, for a considerable length of time.

Possibly an unknown creature which has since become extinct, or only a story?

After this length of time it is hard to tell, but many sightings of monster which have been thought fictitious have been proven as fact, if often distorted fact. As an example, here is how the Portuguese explorer Cadamosto described the West Africans' reaction to a sailing ship:

*It is asserted that when for the first time they saw sails, that is, ships, on the sea (which neither they nor their forefathers had ever seen before) they believed that they were great sea-birds with white wings, which were flying...*

To the comparatively sophisticated Portuguese, this was amusing, but then, they knew what ships were. How many other sea monsters could be explained away by a little knowledge?

Odysseus, the Greek navigator, was warned by Circe to avoid Scylla and Charybdis. In legend, Scylla was a sea monster with twelve feet and six heads. Below her waist she was shaped like a pack of dogs and whenever a ship dared enter the Strait of Messina between Italy and Sicily, each head would snatch a seaman from his rowing bench. It is unlikely that such a creature ever did confront passing mariners, but this section of the Strait does contain some exotic marine life.

Here, deep water currents carry sealife into the shallow strait, where they are frequently stranded, dying, on the surrounding beaches. To people used to upper-level fish, these creatures would indeed be monsters. Here there are swordfish and squid, jellyfish, viperfish and octopus. Perhaps a combination of these exotic animals and the treacherous tidal currents in an otherwise nearly tideless sea was responsible for the mysterious Scylla – and the twelve feet were the arms of an octopus?

Charybdis – the 'sucker down' – is easily explained as a whirlpool; the Corryvreckan off the west coast of Scotland has similar legends of a goddess, which hauled vessels underwater. This was the Cailleach, and the seething white foam of the disturbance was said to be her hair. Norse legend claimed that a goddess, who was doomed to grind salt on the bed of the ocean until the end of time, also created the Swilkie or Swelkie whirlpool in the Pentland Firth. If she ever felt lonely she could have travelled north to the Maelstrom, where another goddess shared her fate.

Squids and octopuses, however, may be responsible for many of the monstrous sea tales. Both these creatures are malevolent, hunting other living things for food, and some have been known to attack man.

In the mid 1930s, it appeared that a plague of sea monsters had arrived off California. Fishermen found their bait had disappeared, their lines were snapped, their catches down. Large squids were responsible for all this, and when the fishermen hauled them in, the squids proved aggressive, biting with their horny beaks and squirting black ink.

Of all squids the largest is the *Architeuthis*, which inhabits the North Atlantic. One specimen caught off Newfoundland was measured at fifty-five feet in length – longer than most vessels in the early sailing days. If the Norsemen in their longboats had come across an animal of this size, they would have been justified in thinking it dangerous. Hence their legends of the Kraken.

In the early years of the $20^{th}$ century, the people of the South Pacific told of a monster octopus that roamed the ocean between the Gilbert Islands and Samoa. Apparently this thing had tentacles about nine feet in length and as thick as the waist of a man.

Then, in 1986, horror became reality. By this time the old colonial powers had gone, taking their names with them and the Gilbert Islands had become Kiribati. Two men were out fishing when the long, suckered, tentacles reached from the depths. Both men were dragged under, and neither was seen again.

What makes this story so tragic is the fact that the young men of these islands used to hunt the octopus for fun. One youth would dive down to where the octopus was known to live and let it enfold him with its tentacles. At that point a second youth would jerk both man and octopus to the surface where he killed it with a single bite between the eyes.

This proves the old adage that one man's monster is another man's dinner.

A year after the Kiribati incident, a trawlerman decided to scour the ocean bed off Bermuda for large crabs. The idea was perfectly sound; the deeper the trawl, the larger would be the crab.

At first the project proceeded perfectly as edible crabs two feet wide were produced, but then the trawlerman began to lose his traps, and his line was snapped. When sonar indicated that some creature 50 feet in height was grappling the trap, the trawlerman became interested. When this thing began to tow his boat, interest altered to concern. Unfortunately the beast released the trap before it could be identified, but the local fishermen suspected a giant octopus had been disturbed.

There have been instances when such creatures have attacked ships.

In the early 1930s, a giant squid in the South Pacific rammed the tanker *Brunswick* of 15000 tons. The officer of the watch, Arne Groenningsaeter, reported the animal as thirty feet long and travelling at more than twelve knots. Groenningsaeter believed that the squid mistook his ship for a sperm whale, its natural enemy.

Sixty years previously, the Times reported on the sinking of the 150-ton schooner *Pearl* by a squid. This was in the Bay of Bengal and the skipper of *Pearl* was the aggressor, shooting at the creature with a rifle.

After that it was a one sided encounter,

> *...the oblong body was at least half the size of our vessel in length and just as thick...the brute struck us, and the ship quivered under the thud...monstrous arms like trees seized the vessel and she heeled over...the brute, holding on by his arms, slipped his vast body overboard and pulled the vessel down.*

There were a few survivors, but what a tale to tell the grandchildren!

The shark is not so much a monster as a killer. In the days of the old Navy, and quite probably still today, bathing parades at sea were always attended by a man constantly on the lookout for sharks.

In 1843 Joseph Stratton was a seaman on board HMS *Samarang* in the East Indies. He spoke of a bathing parade that was interrupted by a shark attack. Everyone

> *...swam to the ropes, which were thrown in every direction...one of the marines who was last, was actually touched by the shark...*

Once they were out of the water, the Navy's tradition of not being defeated asserted itself and the shark was caught and dragged inboard. There it was cut up by the seamen and '...the quivering flesh thrown into the frying pan and eaten with a savage pleasure.'

A shark is a dangerous creature, but were the seamen not just as dangerous? After all, they killed and ate it. Perhaps humans at sea are just as monstrous as any natural marine creature.

Anyway, Sir Francis Chichester has a very sensible comment on sharks in his book *Along the Clipper Way*:

> *As I see it, the only security against a man-eating shark is to avoid being in the sea when the shark is there.*

Horrific though they are, sharks, squid and octopus are all recognisable. It is the thing which cannot be identified which truly fascinates, for those are the creatures of the night, the things once spoken of in the quiet watches when the sea stretched dark to an unseen horizon and the stars were big and close and friendly. Then the imagination had space to roam and something to catch, to expand, and to explore. Then things were seen.

Things like that experienced by the cook of *Noreen*, 120 miles off Bermuda in 1959. 'He had a large body and a small alligator like head.' And when *Noreen* sailed away '...the queer fellow surfaced on our starboard beam.' After a while, in which the thing seemed to be watching them, amused, it slid away.

The North Atlantic seems to possess many strange, or at least uncatalogued, creatures, for off the Cornish coast lives Morgawr, a salt water version of the Loch Ness Monster. In the mid 1970s this was described as

> *...an elephant waving its trunk, but the trunk was a long neck with a small head on the end, like a snake's head...the colour was black and very dark brown, and the skin seemed to be like a sealion's.*

Not the sort of beast to meet while out swimming.

Nor was the creature sighted by the German submarine U28 in the First World War.

> *...it was about 60 feet long, like a crocodile in shape and had four limbs with powerful webbed feet and a long tail tapering to a point.*

This monster – if it was a monster – only came to the surface when U28 torpedoed a British merchant ship. Possibly the underwater explosion lifted it – so again it was man who disturbed the animal, rather than the animal attacking man.

Yet for all that, for all the mythology and horror and folklore, relatively few people are killed by sea creatures. Certainly more die in car accidents, probably more by accidental drowning. And the creature that kills more people at sea than any other is neither squid nor shark nor an unidentified 'thing'. It is the quiet, unheralded jellyfish.

This brainless ... a plant than an animal and
... t. While the common flying
... h worse. Able to grow up to
... ng, it inhabits the seas off
... nan in minutes.

... werful sting, the predatory
... frail whaleboat to pieces,
... and the shore crab which
... e a very dangerous place
... monster.

# 4 The Pirates

In the year 1720 the pirate captains Taylor and England attacked the East Indiaman *Cassandra* of 380 tons, commanded by Captain Macrae. It was unusual for a merchant ship to resist a pirate attack but the stubbornness that had seen Macrae clamber from Ayrshire cottager to East India captain refused to let him surrender.

Rather than a bloodless victory, Taylor and England had to fight for their prize and even when Macrae beached in the Comoro Islands he was able to bargain for his freedom. The go-between was an ex-shipmate of Macrae's, a '...man with a terrible pair of whiskers and a wooden leg.'

Although Macrae was justly rewarded for his courage, it was the wooden legged man who probably gave more to the folklore of piracy, for it is possible that Robert Louis Stevenson reincarnated this character as the genial ruffian Long John Silver in *Treasure Island*. And Long John is probably the epitome of a pirate as imagined by today's world.

A big man, bearing the scars of battle on his body, likeable and jovial but with strong undercurrents of violence, Long John seemed to carry adventure on his shoulders. Yet, just how correct is this picture of a pirate?

There were jovial pirates just as there were cruel pirates and although many would be scarred by battle, many more died of disease and shipwreck. And if Hollywood has placed piracy in the 17$^{th}$ and 18$^{th}$ century Caribbean, the reality infested all seas, pre-dated Christ by many hundreds of years and still continues.

But what exactly is a pirate? To the 16$^{th}$ century Spaniards, Francis Drake and his ilk were pirates, while to the English they were heroes. As Drake worked with the approval of his sovereign, it is probably more accurate to call him a privateer – a private seaman licensed to fight and raid in his country's wars.

Pirates proper had no such licence. They were freebooting sea ruffians who attacked whichever ship or settlement they chose; criminals, plunderers whose roving life gave that appearance of romantic freedom which appeared to either the adventurous or the unprincipled.

In 1600 BC the pirates who preyed on Persian shipping in the Arabian Gulf probably thought of themselves as patriots. The swarms of Sea People who migrated to Palestine in the 12th century BC were in all likelihood considered pirates by the Israelites, Canaanites and Egyptians who suffered from their attacks. In the second century AD the west coast of India was named The Pirate Coast by Ptolemy.

The Sea People certainly had some of the characteristics of pirates; they robbed and plundered and killed. Yet they are too far back in time to have contributed much to our stock of nautical folklore.

The pirates of folklore are men like Captain John Ward who gave a rousing speech before he went a-pirating in 1601:

> *...where are the days that have been, and the seasons that we have seen, where we might sing, swear, drink, drab and kill men as freely as your cake-makers do flies...when the whole sea was our Empire, where we robb'd at will...I tell you if I should met mine own father at sea, I would rob him, and sell him when I had done.*

Captain Ward was described as short, balding, foul mouthed and drunk. He sailed to what was probably one of the most notorious pirate coasts of all time, that of North Africa, and became one of the Barbary Corsairs.

These supposedly Moslem freebooters hunted the Mediterranean for their prey, attacking in long, light and crowded galleys to overpower their victims by a combination of manpower and ferocity. As likely to seek out slaves as treasure, the corsairs clashed with their Christian rivals, the Knights of Rhodes, and later of Malta, in bloody affrays.

Their way of life attracted many renegade Europeans of whom Ward was only one, and these taught the corsairs how to sail and maintain the more seaworthy 'round ships' – the square rigged vessels of north European waters. With these the corsairs could expand their operations, and in 1627 under Murad Rais – a Dutchman whose real name was Jan Janz – they grabbed 400 people from Reykjavik in Iceland. Around the same time a corsair was chased from Shetland waters by a Scandinavian warship and in 1631 Baltimore in Ireland was raided. Ironically, Baltimore was a known pirate haunt.

Scottish folklore tells of an Edinburgh man who was captured by corsairs but rose to command a ship and returned to marry his childhood sweetheart. Although this story is probably apocryphal, it does reveal what was a historical possibility.

In 1615 four Leith seamen were captured and sold in the Algiers slave market. Scotland's social conscience was stirred and the Privy Council ordered a collection in all the kirks to help pay their ransom. There was another collection within a decade as *Lion of Leith* was also pirated.

With a long seaboard and small, scattered communities, the west coast of

Scotland would appear to have been a natural target for the corsairs, but there are no raids remembered. Perhaps a combination of inclement weather and the defensive capabilities of the locals kept this particular scourge away. However, there are many mentions of piracy, both native and foreign, in Scottish waters.

The west coast had the Hebrideans who operated from their island bases with the lymphad. This was a square sailed galley with anything up to thirty six oars and a heavily armed crew who depended on speed, manoeuvrability and boarding to overcome their opponents. Sometimes alone, often in packs, these galleys hunted from Shetland to the Irish Sea, taking merchant shipping or raiding on land as it suited them.

Fishing boats from the east coast or the Netherlands were a favourite target but probably the best known Hebridean pirate was MacNeil of Barra whose capture of English shipping angered Elizabeth I and nearly created a diplomatic rift.

On the east coast the pirates were frequently English or Dutch but in the early 16$^{th}$ century piracy received a serious check thanks to the endeavours of Andrew Wood and the Barton family. Indeed one of the Bartons sent King James IV the gift of a barrel full of pirate heads, pickled in brine.

The last known pirate in Scottish waters was hanged at Leith as late as 1822.

For all that, it is the pirates who infested the seas in the late 17$^{th}$ and early 18$^{th}$ centuries that are best remembered, and most often portrayed.

This was the age of Bartholomew Roberts, of Kidd and Tew and England, of Long Ben Avery and the awesome Blackbeard Teach. These were the men who created the legends and the lore. Yelling devils leaping over the taffrail, treasure buried on remote cays, the black flag, and men marooned on deserted islands, or forced to walk the plank.

Although Chaucer mentions plank-walking, the only known pirate to use this method of ridding himself of unwanted prisoners was Stede Bonnet. And he was caught eventually, and hanged in Charleston, South Carolina, in 1718.

The swift assault and board was common practice for pirates the world over, so much so that Spanish galleons were known to stud their hulls with nails and smear grease on their decks. In this century British merchantmen in the Far East kept their steam hoses handy for similar reasons.

Marooning was a common punishment, putting a disobedient crewman, or an unpopular captain, ashore on a remote island or a deserted piece of mainland. Alexander Selkirk, the original Robinson Crusoe, was treated in this manner and Stevenson used the memory in *Treasure Island* with Ben Gunn.

When William Damper was marooned on the Nicobar Islands he built himself a boat and sailed to freedom, but he was an exceptional man. Other men either died, or survived as Selkirk did.

Buried treasure is one of the more enduring pirate myths and one of the hardest to prove. For if the existence of buried treasure could be ascertained – by a map, for instance – somebody would go and dig it up. However, the famous Captain Kidd certainly buried at least part of his hoard in Gardiner's Island, at Boston. That was recovered by the authorities, but rumour and speculation insisted that there was much more, either left on board his ship *Quedah Merchant* or elsewhere beneath the rich North American soil. One story claims that Kidd rowed ashore on *Hispaniola* and buried his brass bound chest. Either he worked alone or else cold-bloodedly killed his helpers, for there was no trust between Kidd and his rabble of a crew.

The black flag was also genuine, although occasionally it was red. French seamen named this the 'pretty red' flag – the 'jolie rouge' that became corrupted to Jolly Roger. In the pirate settlements of the West Indies there were women who made a living by making these flags, sometimes even decorating them with the romantic skull and crossbones motif. Not that those seamen who saw it flutter from the masthead of an approaching ship would think it romantic.

Horrifying would be a better description. Or terrifying. The black flag denoted no quarter. Death.

If this flag was not worn the victim's crew could heave to and submit to being robbed of anything valuable. Often the pirates would question the crew about their treatment and take summary vengeance on a brutal captain or officer. Frequently some or all of the crew would be invited to join the pirate ship.

If the pirates were simple sea-robbers out for plunder it was probably more sensible to surrender than to fight. On the other hand there were some truly terrible people out beyond the horizon and if they targeted a ship 'Them that die'll be the lucky ones' as Long John Silver declared.

There was Montbars, known as 'The Exterminator' who had the romantic pastime of nailing a man's intestines to the mast before thrusting a burning torch against his behind so he ran round the deck to a sickening and bloody death. Or the Frenchman Jean David Nau, known as Llonnais, who once decapitated the entire crew of a frigate, licking the blood from his blade after each death. He was also depicted chewing on a human heart he had just removed from its rightful owner.

And there was the Dutchman Roche-Brazilian who spitted Spaniards alive and roasted them over a fire.

A ghoulish crew, and British pirates could be every bit as bad. When Captain Edward Low witnessed a merchant captain throw his money into the sea rather than wait to be robbed, he took savage revenge. Cutting off the man's lips, he had them boiled and forced his victim to eat them, before killing both him and his crew. Another captain was tortured by having lighted slowmatches placed between his fingers, and yet another was forced to eat his own ears.

Of all these psychopaths, one of the best to avoid, but most colourful, was Blackbeard Teach. Like so many seamen, Teach hailed from Bristol and sailed to the hunting grounds of the Caribbean, basing himself at the pirate colony of New Providence in the Bahamas, then at Bath, North Carolina. A contemporary provided a description of him:

> *This beard was black, which he suffered to grow of an extraordinary length; as to breadth it came up to his eyes. He was accustomed to twist it with ribbons, in small tails...and turn them about his ears. In times of action he wore a sling over his shoulders, with three brace of pistols, laying in holsters, like bandoliers; and stuck lighted matches under his hat, which, appearing on each side of his face, his eyes naturally looking fierce and wild, made him altogether such a figure that imagination cannot form an idea of a Fury from Hell to look more frightful.*

Or more vain, perhaps?

Obviously formidable to opponents, Blackbeard was equally dangerous to befriend. One of his party tricks was to fire pistols beneath the table during a card game. Another, to have a gathering in the hold, batten down the hatches and light barrels of sulphur. Last man to cry 'enough!' was the winner. Blackbeard never lost.

The last of his fourteen wives was a child of sixteen and once he had bedded her Blackbeard insisted that half a dozen of his crew enjoy her carnal delights as he watched.

Even his drinking habits were unusual; he invented a lethal cocktail that he named rumfustian; rum and sherry, beer and gin, laced with gunpowder. However, justice caught him when his depredations began to affect the tobacco merchants of Virginia. The Governor sent out ships that hunted him down and killed him. The Governor's name was Spottiswood and his grandfather had been the Archbishop of St Andrews, so he possibly had a hereditary understanding of villainy.

Seen beside Blackbeard, Long John Silver seems almost benign, but if the character was fictitious the name was borrowed from possibly the most ambitious of all pirates – Long Ben Avery.

Long Ben was also known as John, or sometimes Henry Avery. A Plymouth man, son and brother of sea captains and ship owners, he learned his trade in Pepys' navy, continued as mate in a family ship and gained experience in both the West Indies and the slave trade.

In 1693, at the age of 38, Long Ben was refused the command of one of his family ships and perhaps this knockback changed an adventurous seaman into an out and out rogue. But the passage to piratehood was crooked. Long Ben became first mate of a ship with the patriotic name of *Charles II*, which was leased to Spain. Although *Charles II* was intended for the Peruvian coast, she had reached only as far as Corunna before the crew mutinied, sent their drunken captain ashore and appointed Long Ben as their new commander.

A mutineer and a pirate, there was no turning back. Renaming the 46 gun ship *Fancy,* Long Ben slipped south, round the Cape of Good Hope and anchored in St Mary's, Madagascar, one of the pirate havens.

From here Fancy sailed north, gathering allies on the way, including the Rhode Islander Captain Tew. In a six-strong pirate flotilla Long Ben captured *Futteh Mahmood* with a cargo of gold and silver valued at tens of thousands of pounds.

That was an excellent start, but then came one of the most valuable ships ever to cross the bows of a pirate. This was the Great Mogul's own ship *Gunj Guwani* which name translates as 'exceeding treasure' but the best of the treasure could not be counted in gold. Despite her 80 guns and hundreds of soldiers, she fell victim to Long Ben.

There was treasure to the value of at least £350,000, but there was also a bevy of ladies from the court of Aurangzeb himself, the Great Mogul. Legend says that his mother-in-law was on board, and sealore tells of the suicide of some high bred ladies. No wonder, after being subjected to the vicious pleasures of the women hungry, unscrupulous and probably unwashed pirates.

A persistent tale says that one of the ladies was the daughter of Aurangzeb and Long Ben took her for himself. His intention was to wed her and bed her and place a boy of Avery blood on the throne of Delhi.

Although this never happened, his crew received £1000 a man and when *Fancy* arrived at New Providence, Long Ben shipped to England.

Here legend takes over. Perhaps Avery fell into bad company in Bristol and was robbed of his hard stolen wealth. Perhaps he did marry the Indian princess and together they ruled a happy land in Madagascar.

Long Ben shares in history the part Long John occupies in fiction. Both were rascals, both were dangerous, but both are men who intrigue. There is a tendency to wish them well, as long as they remain well away from us.

But that is the essential lure of pirate lore. They were rogues, with their egalitarian lifestyle of freedom and adventure, fascinating while they remain in fiction or in the past. But if Long John, or Long Ben, or God forbid, Edward Low or Montbars, came over our horizon, all thought of romance and fascination would vanish.

Better to keep them between the pages of a book.

*Inscription at Durban Harbour, Baffin Island, left by the whaler* Joseph Green *in 1837.* Reproduced by permission of Aberdeenshire Heritage.

*'hale alongside the* Eclipse *(1880s).* Reproduced by permission of Aberdeenshire Heritage.

# 5 Famous Ships

Many ships have achieved fame, yet there are relatively few whose name has lived long in memory. To the ordinary man in the street – whoever he is – there are perhaps twenty, maybe fewer than a dozen famous ships, although the names will alter from person to person.

Many will name Noah's *Ark*, most will have heard of *Titanic* and while English people might know of *Golden Hinde* and *Great Eastern,* Scots may mention *Comet* or *Great Michael.*

Without doubt Noah's *Ark* was the world's first floating zoo. But although we tend to think of the *Ark* as being exclusive to Noah, and represent her as an ugly, clumsy thing shaped like a house on a high hull, neither of these conceptions seems correct.

In *The Histories* by Tacitus, one chapter describes a civil war in the eastern Mediterranean and the Black Sea. Conditions had deteriorated until:

> *Even the uncivilised natives insolently roved the seas in hastily constructed boats. These they call arks: they are narrow above the waterline, but broad in the beam and neither bronze nor iron rivets is used in their construction. When the sea is choppy, they increase the freeboard by adding planks successively according to the height of the waves, until they are wholly enclosed by a sort of roof. In this fashion they ride the waves. Identical in shape fore and aft the boats can be rowed in both directions since it does not matter whether they are beached stern or bow first: either way is equally safe.*

Compare that to the construction of Noah's *Ark* in Genesis chapter six. 'So make yourself an ark of cypress wood; make rooms in it and coat it with pitch inside and out...make a roof for it and finish the ark to within 18 inches (a cubit) of the top...'

Not identical but similar; coating a boat with pitch was necessary in the warm Mediterranean; for otherwise the ship-boring worms would perforate the hull and create all manner of problems.

But what were the sailing qualities of such a vessel?

Noah would be the best person to ask, or Captain Fife of *Golden Fleece.*

When this clipper was launched in 1869, her designer claimed that she had the same proportions as Noah's *Ark*. She had high praise from Captain Fife who said she could do everything but talk and could nearly steer herself. She was also fast; 72 days from London to Sydney, 13 days across the Atlantic.

So the ark was not the clumsy, ugly brute of so many pictures but a graceful, extremely seaworthy vessel. Perhaps her designer knew more about things maritime than is generally accepted.

There is a huge gulf in time between the ark and James IV's great *Michael*, but not so great a gulf as in their function. While the ark was designed to save and maintain, *Michael* was built to enhance the prestige of a king and to blow his enemies out of the water.

It was 1511 and Scotland's energetic king intended building a navy which would impress Europe. Pride of the fleet would be *Michael*, largest ship in the world and flagship of a crusade against the Turks. Whatever he was, James IV was not a man for petty dreams. A deepwater site was needed, for Leith had a sandbar across the harbour entrance so an entire village was built for the scores of craftsmen and wrights from Spain and France, Flanders and Denmark, and for the hundreds of local labourers. First a breakwater was built, then docks, ropewalk and warehouses were added to this new haven on the Forth.

If contemporary or near contemporary accounts are to be believed, she was huge. Europe was scoured for the best possible materials and Scotland poured in her talent and hacked down her forests. The not always accurate historian Pitscottie gives her a length of 240 feet, a breadth of 56 and hull planking 10 feet thick. Strong enough to withstand the cannonball that the king fired to test her out.

French influence may have made her carvel-built with gunports for the 32 cannon in her hull. French influence could have given her lateen sails on the after two of her four masts. But it was purely Scottish for the king to buy strawberries for the little local girl he guided round the dockyard and purely Scottish for the king to adze the planking in person and join the local fishermen at the oysterbeds. Scottish too for the locals to brawl with the foreign craftsmen.

In 1511 this splendid, clumsy, majestic vessel was launched on the Forth. In 1513 she went to war sailing with 8 or10 other Scottish ships, northabout through the Pentland Firth. Capturing Carrickfergus from its English garrison on the way, the Scottish fleet sailed to France.

*Michael* never returned. Either she was burned or she just rotted away at her moorings. This wasteful fate also befell *Golden Hinde*, the ship used by Francis Drake on his epic voyage round the world.

When Drake sailed her out of Plymouth in 1577 she was named *Pelican,* a neat, seaworthy, 18-gun vessel of three masts and around 100 tons. In the South Atlantic there was mutiny and Drake executed one Thomas Doughty, one time secretary to the Earl of Essex. After that *Pelican's* name was changed.

A golden hind was the crest of Sir Charles Hatton, captain of Queen Elizabeth's guard and a courtier who had helped finance this voyage. No doubt Drake felt that after killing one gentleman it would be politic to compliment another; a friend at court was always useful.

On the other hand it was considered unlucky to change the name of a ship; soon after the renaming of *Pelican* a 52-day-long storm blew up, together with a lunar eclipse. *Marigold*, consort of *Golden Hinde*, was lost with all hands. It was now that Drake was driven south of Tierra Del Fuego and accidentally discovered the passage since named in his honour.

It was 1580 before Drake returned to England, with one ship remaining of his squadron but enough honour to blazon English seamanship across the world and enough booty to make his crew incredibly rich.

*Golden Hinde* was kept on display at Deptford, where she remained until rot destroyed her. Yet her memory remains and in 1973 a replica was built, as near to the original as possible. The new *Golden Hinde* has also circumnavigated the globe, and her crew lived as did their predecessors.

If *Golden Hinde* wakened the world to the oncoming sea might of England, it was a comet which alerted mariners of the approaching transformation of sea transport.

'Steam kettles', seamen called the graceless little vessels with their clumsy paddles and filthy funnels, their perpetual pall of smuts, their hissing, spurting steam and clattering machinery. *Experiment* had been an attempt at a muscle-powered paddleboat; eleven hours of failure on the Forth as the crazy contraption slogged it out with the waves. Then came Miller and Symington's effort on Dalswinton Loch, and finally *Charlotte Dundas* on the Forth and Clyde canal.

This was success on inland water – now steam came to the sea. Designed by Henry Bell, built by John Wood of Port Glasgow, the 40-foot steamboat remained anonymous until a flaring comet inspired a name. Only then did her entire four-horse power churn onto the Clyde.

Despite the maroon sofas in her cabin, the library for the learned and the mirror for the vain, *Comet* ran aground at Renfrew and it was Mrs Bell who encouraged the passengers to help push her off the inconvenient sandbank.

For the Clyde, *Comet* pointed a golden finger, albeit grimy with soot, into the shipbuilding future, but for the hardy men of the sailing ships, her maiden voyage was the smudged thumbprint of a long and ultimately terminal decline.

In 1820 *Comet* became the world's first ocean-going steamboat as Donald MacDougall piped her through the Crinan Canal and up to Oban. Yet, as if to reveal the pain of passing sail, the ocean turbulence of Dorus Mor, the Great

Door between Jura and Scarba pulled *Comet* onto the rocks of Craignish Point. In a sleety storm on December 12th, *Comet* ended her career. But she had shown the way.

In her wake came many strange vessels, and one of the most inspired steamship designers was the Portsmouth born Isambard Kingdom Brunel. He is probably best remembered for his *Great Eastern*, for which the prefix 'great' is, if anything, an understatement. Built in Millwall in 1858, this vessel held the accolade of the world's largest for a full forty years.

Even today, her statistics are impressive. She had accommodation for 4000 passengers, or 10,000 troops, She could hold 12,000 tons of coal and 6000 tons of cargo: Brunel intended building a ship large enough to sail to Australia without halting to fill her bunkers.

Although she used a combination of sails, paddle wheels and the still developing screws, *Great Eastern* was still underpowered. It was two years before a buyer was found and even then *Great Eastern* was sold at a discount price.

Bad luck sailed with her; her first captain drowned, six men died in an explosion and she was described as the ugliest ship that ever sailed.

Only after she was scrapped in 1888 was the skeleton of a man found in her double bottom and superstition claimed that this had caused all her ill luck.

Before *Great Eastern* was Brunel's *Great Britain*, launched in 1843 and a ship once described as the 'forefather of all modern ships'. *Great Britain* was much more successful, both as a passenger carrier and a cargo vessel but in 1886 she became a victim of the Horn. Limping into the Falklands, she proved too expensive to repair, so remained there for eighty years. In 1970 she was brought back to Bristol, where she had been built. Today *Great Britain* can be visited in that very maritime city.

The other ship for which Brunel is famous was *Great Western*. She has been hailed as the first British steamship to cross the Atlantic. Unfortunately this is incorrect; she may have been the first steamship intended for the transatlantic crossing, but *Sirius* of Leith pipped her.

Built by R. Menzies and Sons, *Sirius* weighed 703 tons and was so short of fuel that she had to burn both cabin furniture and spare spars to complete her 18 day passage to New York. *Great Western* arrived less than 24 hours later.

If *Sirius* is barely remembered, her seamen would not complain. They have the compensation of a snug Leith tavern tavern that bears *Sirius* name.

Probably one of the most famous ships in the world, it is doubtful if *Titanic* would be half so well remembered if she had not been sunk by an iceberg. She was built in Belfast for the White Star Line, whose vessels competed with Cunard for North Atlantic passengers, but never for the Blue Riband.

At 46,329 tons she was the largest liner in the world and when she left Southampton on her maiden voyage to New York in April 10th 1912 there were a score of millionaires and over 700 immigrants among the 2201 people on board. There were also squash courts, Turkish baths, three libraries, a gymnasium and a swimming pool; all the luxuries the cream of society had come to demand. It was a long step from *Comet*, one hundred years previously.

At ten o'clock in the evening of Sunday 14th, the second class passengers sang 'Oh hear us when we cry to thee; For those in peril on the sea.'

That same Sunday, *Titanic* was warned at least five times of icebergs ahead, but she continued on her course, virtually unheeding. And at 11:40pm she struck an iceberg. For years it was thought that a hole 300 feet long had been slashed in her hull, now divers have discovered that a number of smaller punctures were made. Either way *Titanic* began to sink.

If she had slowed at the iceberg warning, she might have remained afloat, with the force of impact less and the gashes in her hull smaller, or in less dangerous locations. As it was, six of *Titanic*'s sixteen watertight compartments were holed, and the incoming water quickly pulled her down by the bows.

'CQD' called the radio operator, 'CQD' the international distress call. By 12:20 the bulkheads were collapsing. At 12:30 the order was passed to put women and children in the boats, and stewards were still gently wakening the passengers.

*Carpathia* not too far away, signalled 'Coming hard.'

Many of the crew and most of the passengers were unaware of their lifeboat stations, but the band played ragtime and, after all, *Titanic* was unsinkable.

But nobody had told the sea that.

Lifeboats departed with few people on board; one with 28 rather than 65, another carrying Sir Combo and Lady Duff Gordon and just ten others. Most of the thwarts were empty as an officer punched a panicking immigrant and pistol shots were fired to quell a terrified mass of people

Women were screaming, fainting, as the great screws rose clear of the water, as officers stopped the lower deck passengers from rushing the too-few boats. One woman, refused permission to take her dog into a lifeboat, stepped back onto *Titanic* to drown with her pet. Major Butts waved goodbye to his wife in her lifeboat. Mrs Straus refused to leave her husband: 'We've been together many years; where you go, so will I go'

'Goodbye dear' said Colonel Astor as he put his wife on a boat. 'I'll see you later.'

'Nearer my God to thee' played the band.

'Oh, save me! Save me!' yelled one woman, and a man replied:

'Good lady, save yourself; only God can save you now.'

There were terrible scenes in the water. A woman punching at a drowning man as he tried to clamber into her lifeboat; another woman helping him inboard as the blood from the ringcuts on his face dribbled into the icy water. Men and women were using their oars to fend off hopeful swimmers. Men drowning; and only then was the iceberg seen, blue white in the night.

1494 people drowned.

There was no Birkenhead drill aboard *Titanic* and she is remembered as a doomed ship rather than the most luxurious liner of her day.

Why were so many mistakes made on that night? There are many theories, and the full truth will never be known. But *Titanic* is certainly recalled as a famous ship.

# 6 Mermaids

Until the advent of political correctness, mermaids were fairly frequently found in children's books. Usually they were cute creatures who combed their flowing blonde hair while perched on a rock. Copenhagen has a mermaid similar to this, as has the Wellgate Centre in Dundee. They were harmless, of course, and friendly, but the old time seamen did not view them like this at all.

To seamen, the merfolk were seen as some sort of supernatural being, not quite a spirit of the sea for they were of solid flesh, but dangerous to know and best avoided. In Britain they were most commonly met on the coasts of northern Scotland, Galloway and the south west of England. Areas with strong maritime connections but also remote from the main population centres. Perhaps merfolk were more widespread until humankind pushed them back.

Seemingly merfolk did not live at sea but in the caves gouged by the sea in coastal cliffs. Around 1830 the mighty cliffs at the Bullers of Buchan were home to a mermaid and some of the local people held conversations with her. That was a daring act, for not long before a mermaid who sat with her tail coiled round the bowsprit had guided a Peterhead ship onto rocks. All the crew died in the subsequent wreck, except the man who staggered ashore with the news. Perhaps the mermaid let him live, to continue the legend?

They were sirens, these creatures, and lured ships to destruction with their songs while they beguiled men with their beauty. The Corryvreckan disturbance between Jura and Scarba is said to be home to a mermaid, but surely her melodies would be ignored. No seaman from the days of sail would willingly venture there, with that powerful suction.

But the folklore of mermaids has a romantic twist with the bittersweet quality so familiar in relationships doomed by fate. There are the mermaid tears, for instance, the lovely little pebbles found on the beaches of Iona.

According to the story, once there was a mermaid who fell in love with an Abbot of that island, but because of his holy calling and her lack of a soul, her love was both unfulfilled and rejected. But when she cried, her tears were changed into these pebbles.

Many mermaids also had a romantic interest in the young men of the west, and their demand for human lovers was insatiable.

In the wild seas beyond Duncansby Head there lived a particularly man-hungry mermaid and she hunted the coasts and islands of the north for handsome men to furnish her home. Rather than sing, this mermaid preyed on man's greed and offered pearls and treasure from all the wrecked ships on the seabed.

Once they were captured, the men were dragged to the bottom of the sea and fettered with a golden chain. Dozens of these captives still languish beneath the seas, loved and guarded by the mermaid whose task it is to look after the treasure of the sea god himself.

The old time fishermen in their tiny boats and wide meshed nets would beg forgiveness of any mermaid they inadvertently hauled up in their nets. Then they would let her go, for mermaids, however beautiful, invariably brought bad luck. There were very few exceptions.

Yet there was one occasion when good came of an association between man and mermaid.

About 150 years ago there was a boat builder in Wester Ross named Roderick Mackenzie. He was a skilled craftsman and always took time to find the best materials for the clinker built vessels he built. The best lengths of wood, the finest nails, the straightest oars and masts. He wanted his boats to dance on the wild seas of the west and was saddened when sometimes they sank and the tide brought home the pale corpses of the crew.

Then one day he came across a mermaid. She was alone and out of the water so he grabbed her. Although she struggled, and her long tail was slippery and wickedly strong, he held her down until, eventually she began to weep and beg to be released.

'Certainly,' said Mackenzie, 'I'll let you back in the sea on one condition – that nobody will ever be drowned from a boat that I build.'

With a mixture of frustration and relief the mermaid agreed and from that time on Mackenzie's boats were much sought after in the west. And nobody ever drowned from them.

In the south west of England, a mermaid went by the name of a sea-morgan and although the details were different, the characteristics were similar. Like the Scottish variety, the merfolk of the Severn were best avoided.

Somewhere in Somerset's Bridgewater Bay there lived a very beautiful sea-morgan that gilded the evening air with her singing. Many men were enchanted by her lovely voice and ventured closer, but the morgan lived in a quicksand. Struggling in the sand, the men would yell for help, only to see the cold eyes and sharp teeth of the conger eels that slithered toward them. Hearing the bark of the eels, the siren call of the morgan, the locals knew that another man had been trapped and eaten. They decided that the sea-morgan had to be removed.

They chose a man who was deaf, and so immune to the music of the morgan. He had been born on a Sunday, the son of a witch. As was well known, those Sunday-born are immune to the supernatural evil of a sea-morgan, while having a witch-mother, it was thought, might also create some sympathetic magic.

This man used a mud sledge to slide on top of the quicksand and when the conger eels congregated around him, he killed a dozen with his eel spear. Just as he was closing in on the morgan, she screamed loudly and vanished. She was never seen again.

There are many tales of mermaids, under various names; so many that there may be some truth, however deeply buried. Perhaps there once was a people with partially webbed feet – people born that way in north east Scotland were believed immune from drowning – or perhaps a memory of a vanished race of sea rovers? People who haunted the coasts in prehistoric times, shellfish gatherers who lived in seaside caves and whose memory became distorted by time?

The whistle of wind through cave and round rock would be changed to melodic singing by the superstitious. A charm of song to tempt the unwary into dangerous waters?

Perhaps this Neanderthal race even kidnapped more advanced peoples to keep their numbers up, as the fairy folk were alleged to do – these same fairy folk whose singing enchanted men into captivity.

Yet in the old Norse sagas, the description of a merman is too well defined to be only a vague folk memory. In *The King's Mirror* there is no ambiguity:

> *This monster is tall and of a great size and rises straight out of the water. It has shoulders like a man's but no hands. Its body apparently grows narrower from the shoulders down so that the lower down it has been observed, the more slender it appears to be. But no one has ever seen how the lower end is shaped. No one has ever observed it closely enough to determine whether its body has scales like a fish or skin like a man. Whenever the monster has shown itself, men have always been sure that a storm would follow.*

The last quoted sentence could be the most significant, for scientific opinion now says that this merman could be an optical distortion created by warm air moving over the cool surface of the sea. This occurs before a storm, and could make an isolated rock appear taller, or a marine animal different.

A distorted rock then, and a little imagination.

On the other hand, the mermaid had breasts and long hair, webbed feet and a fish-like tail.

People have suggested that the manatee could be responsible for some of these sightings. This is a tailed mammal with a snout and large flippers. Native to the Caribbean, one might have been caught by the North Atlantic Drift and sighted by the crew of a curragh or longboat. Seen in the trough of a wave, a glimpse of head and tail and flipper would be enough to inflame the imagination of a crew already tense with long voyaging, and a mermaid would be born.

So the merfolk could be a combination of the prehistoric hunter-gatherer who lived in caves along the shore, an optical illusion, wind blowing through rocks and unfamiliar, but quite normal, sea creatures.

So much for the northern European mermaid, but the islands of the East also had their legends of merfolk, again with a different name. This creature was named a 'ri'. Like its northern counterpart, the ri had long hair – dark, not blonde, light skin and breasts.

These ri have been known for centuries but have never been identified. However, the dugong, a herb-eating creature with hand like flukes, could be responsible for the sightings.

Different animals that have helped create a remarkably similar mythology. And sometimes northerners saw a strange creature in the south.

In 1820 James Weddell was on a sealing and exploring voyage in the deep South Atlantic when one of his crew claimed to see a mermaid. This was at Hall Island. The creature was reddish in colour, had a human head with long green hair and a tail like a seal. Weddell entered the sighting in his log with little comment.

Then there were the mermaids of the Queen Charlotte Islands.

Here, off the Pacific coast of Canada, lived the Haida people who enjoyed a wealth of folklore. One of their stories is remarkably similar to tales told in Scotland and if nothing else this reveals the essential similarity between the peoples of the world beneath the fragile veneer of race, colour or language.

One day a Haida family was paddling along the coast in their canoe when they grew tired and landed on a beach. Almost at once the man, who was a shaman and wise in these matters, noticed the track of a devil-fish on the sand, and saw a stockpile of devil-fish food.

Knowing how dangerous these things could be, the Haida man decided to hunt and kill the devil-fish. However the creature had been watching and it struck first. Emerging from its cave, it grabbed the man and dragged him away.

For a while the Haidan wife searched for her missing husband but as there was no sign she concluded that he had been killed. She paddled away with her two children.

But the man was not dead. The devil-fish was a female and had taken him back to the chief of the devil-fish folk, who just happened to be her father. After a while the man grew used to his captivity and he fell in love with the devil-fish who had captured him.

They were married and for years lived as man and wife but all the time the man wondered what had happened to his human wife and children. Gathering his courage he approached the devil-fish chief and asked to leave. After some persuasion the devil-fish chief agreed.

With the Haidan man paddling one canoe and his devil-fish wife another, they moved quickly along the coast. When they came to the village of the man's father they were welcomed for they had brought treasure from devil-fish land.

In time, with astute trading, the man became an important chief and was visited by his human children. To celebrate his return he held first one feast and then another. Five in all and his human wife and his devil-fish wife were present at each.

But as the man had been homesick, so was the devil-fish wife. She missed the life of the sea and one day, in front of her husband, she slipped between the planks of the floor and vanished. Unwilling to lose his second wife, the Haida man followed, changing into a devil-fish as they swam together back to their chosen home.

*Whalers in Lerwick harbour.* Reproduced by permission of Aberdeenshire Heritage.

# 7 Nicknames

Seamen and those associated with the sea seem to have a genius for attaching nicknames to people, objects and places. Everything from the personal eccentricities of a ship's captain to the perceived characteristics of a coast attracts a name.

This last has produced some interesting and highly evocative names, such as the famous Spanish Main. Even to mouth that phrase conjures up images of bright parrots, one-legged pirates and the galleons of Spain. Although the entire Central American coastline has been included in this name, technically it should apply only to that portion of the coast between the mouth of the Orinoco and the Isthmus of Panama. To the Spanish, this coast was Tierra Firma, although the shores of Venezuela were known as the Pearl Coast in the late 16th century.

The deep-water seamen of the 19th century termed the Pacific coast of South America as, bluntly, the West Coast, but to get there they had to round Cape Horn. This notorious place was 'The Horn' or 'Cape Stiff'. Other Cape Stiffs included Good Hope, Leeuwin in Western Australia and Guardafui in Somaliland.

Africa invited these nautical names. There was the Barbary Coast that stretched along the southern shore of the Mediterranean and held those predatory sea people the Barbary Corsairs. This term sometimes included the continuance of the coast past the Pillars of Hercules to western Morocco, where the Gallee Rovers sailed from the port of Gallee near Rabat, adding their quota of mayhem to the seas.

Further south was the Grain Coast. The grain was Guinea pepper, sometimes known as the Grains of Paradise. Then came the Ivory Coast, which still retains its name, and the Gold Coast, which gave its name to a colony, now the nation of Ghana. Further east was the Slave Coast, a name of shame which speaks for itself and an area which was frequented by European and American seamen for hundreds of fateful years. This coast extended from the Volta River to Mount Cameroon.

Central to all this was the Bight of Benin, where the ghoulish rhyme originated:

*Beware and take care of the Bight of Benin*
*Where one comes out for forty goes in.*

To the seamen this was a fever coast, a ghastly, terrible place of malaria and flux, blackwater fever and human degradation. It was here that the black slave traders of the interior brought their collections of captives to the white slave traders from the sea.

In this part of Africa slavery was a way of life; it balanced the economy of many African chiefs and was so prevalent that men and women mutilated themselves to be safe from the slavers. Men like the Kroo-boys, swift surf riders of the coast, who filed their teeth into points to be identified as the indispensable seamen that they were.

When the slave trade ended, ground out of existence by the Royal Navy and the disapproval of a dozen nations, human sacrifice took its place, while palm-oil traders replaced the sleek slaveship. Now the Slave Coast became known as the Coast of Dead Ned.

Naval expeditions pitted the Gatling gun – which the natives had not got – and the cutlasses of the bluejackets against fever and the war bands of tribal chiefs. Appalling places, the tribal strongholds, where pieces of human bodies were festooned amidst the fetish trees, where the ground was saturated with blood and skulls were paraded in their thousands.

If the seaman escaped the fever, there was always dysentery and drink and the offshore islands. Then the fever-weakened men had to face the Atlantic.

Beware and take care...

South again to the Skeleton Coast, where the sea lashes the dunes of the Namib Desert with a never-ending whip of surf and the bleached bones of splintered ships beg pity from a pitiless sun. Then round that other Cape Stiff where Good Hope was often lost amidst the storms. If the temptation to linger at Capetown's Tavern of the Seas was overcome, the seamen faced the Wild Coast of Transkei.

Here high winds clashed with the Mozambique-Aghulis Current to create waves a chilling ninety feet high, crashing in white frothed fury along the continental shelf. In the days when the Dutch, Portugese and British squabbled for Empire, many eastbound ships foundered on this seething shore, and the wondering local tribes succoured shipwrecked fugitives.

Areas of sea also have their nickname. There was the Doldrums, where sailing ships could lie becalmed for days, weeks, with the crew idle and listless, the captain worrying about water and rum and mutiny. The term 'in the doldrums' has passed into the English language.

A total opposite was the 'Roaring Forties', which lie between 40 and 50 degrees south latitude. Here the winds blast from the west and were used extensively by the old sailing captains as they raced their fine ships home. Other winds included the Levanter in the Mediterranean, the northwesterly Chocolate Gale of the Caribbean and the Wolleys, or Willy-Wawa of the high southern latitudes.

In the Atlantic were the Horse Latitudes, around 30 degrees north and south. The story goes that here ships carrying horses to the Americas or Australia were often becalmed and as their water grew short they had to throw the animals overboard. Horses also appear in O'Donohue's White Horses, which are waves with a foaming crest.

If a Cape Buster or a Horn Snorter hit the ship, she might go down to Davy Jones Locker. This $18^{th}$ century nickname for the seabed might come from the Caribbean term 'duppy' for devil, while Jones was a corruption of Jonah. The locker was the grave of drowned seamen. A more simple explanation says that Davy Jones was a pirate and his sea chest, or locker, sank to the bottom.

There were worse devils than Duppy Jonah however. There was Jean Bart, the late $17^{th}$ century privateer who ripped such great gaps in the English merchant fleet that he became 'The French Devil.' Or there was Captain Devil; Simon Danisker, a Dutchman who joined the Algerian corsairs. In two years at the beginning of the $17^{th}$ century he captured 40 ships, yet when he returned to Europe the French welcomed him.

Other pirates were more terrible still. Francois le Clerc was known as Woodenleg by the Spanish – a $16^{th}$ century Long John Silver. A painful wound from a cannonball gave Louis le Golif his name of Half-arse, and Montbars was The Exterminator, a man who enjoyed his killing.

Lord Cochrane of the Royal Navy was termed Le Loupe de Mer, the Sea wolf, by Napoleon Bonaparte after his depredations among French shipping in the Mediterranean. He was nearly as unpopular among his superiors, for he was a man of independent mind, a fiery temper and unique ideas. He was also a superb seaman.

Admiral Byron was known as Foul Weather Jack as he seemed to attract bad weather and, as he failed to find the Northwest Passage, and failed to defeat the French in battle, his luck was foul too. An earlier Admiral, John Norris, had the same epithet, no doubt for similar reasons.

Another searcher for the North west passage was Luke Foxe and he became North West Foxe for his persistence, while Admiral Cornwallis, a man of ruddy complexion, was either Mr Whip or Old Billy-Go-Tight to the hands, although presumably not to his face. Alternatively he was Billy Blue from his habit of flying the Blue Peter when making sail.

Then there was Black Dick, the Earl Howe who won the battle of the 'Glorious First of June' in 1794. He was named, not for his bad temper, but for his dark complexion.

King William was called the Sailor King because of his time as a midshipman.

Other, less pleasant, people said he was Silly Billy, yet in later years he permitted seamen to drink his health sitting down, rather than leaping to their feet and endangering their heads on the low beams of the deck above.

Later in the 19th century, there was Shotgun Murphy, who once thumped his helmsman with a belaying pin, and Shanghai Brown, whose name seems easy to explain. There were the hard-case captains like Jack-the-Devil and Hellfire Jack and many with the prefix of 'Bully' such as Bully Forbes or Bully Waterman. Forbes is mentioned in a sea shanty along with other interesting people such as Boss-eyed Bill the Bowery Bastard; Santander Jim the Frisco Bludger; Sam the Rocket from hell and Joe the Mobile Digger. Even though so much has been remembered, even more has been lost and if all these characters were as genuine as Bully Forbes, there is a wealth of detail, much of it probably gruesome, which would unveil the reality of those days and probably remove the romance completely.

Some of the humour returned in the 20th century, with Potato Jones, Ham and Egg Jones and Corncob Jones. Captain Potato Jones tried to take his steamer *Llewellyn* through Franco's blockade in 1937, but was frustrated by the Royal Navy. Ham and Eggs and Corncob were also blockade-runners of the same war. Brave men.

Another food nickname was Fanny Adams, the Naval term for canned meat; merchant seamen called it Harriet Lane after a woman of that place who was said to be chopped up into small pieces. Then there was 'black pudding' which was what the trainee officers termed the horsewhip used on their persons at the Naval Academy at Gosport.

Burgoo was oatmeal gruel mixed with salted meat, while cracker hash was biscuit soaked in water mixed, again, with salt meat. Unsoftened biscuit was hard tack. There was also the more appetising figgy duff which was steamed suet pudding with dried fruit and Chinese wedding cake, which was rice pudding, dotted with raisins. Babies' Heads was not a dish for cannibals but the more prosaic meal of a small steak and kidney pudding.

Lobscouse was more interesting. Often just a meat stew, it was the main food of the Liverpool packet ships and created the nickname Scouser for the ocean going Liverpudlian. Eventually of course any native of Liverpool could be a Scouse.

Other terms were more general. For instance a midshipman was a 'snotty', who had no pockets for a handkerchief, and brass buttons on his sleeve. Occasionally he was known as a 'wart'. A 'snotty-nurse' was the lieutenant who looked after the gunroom which the midshipmen inhabited. An experienced seaman could be either a shellback or an old salt, while a ship's boy, who carried powder to the cannon during battle, was a powder-monkey.

Many seamen referred to an empty bottle as a marine because without the contents it was useless. Another theory dates back to the late 18th century when the Duke of York ordered the empties cleared from the table. 'Here, take away these marines!' Naturally annoyed, a marine officer asked what the Duke meant. 'They have done their duty' said the Duke, 'and are prepared to do it again.'

A marine could also be a bullock, a grabby, a turkey or a lobster, from the colour of his tunic. Another term was a jolly. A tame-jolly was a militiaman, known less for ferocity in battle than for his garish uniform.

Yet another name for a marine was Mistress Roper, as the marines were as lubberly as women with the ship's ropes. To marry Mistress Roper was to join the marines.

Ropes also had strange names. Each government dockyard inserted a coloured strand into the ropes they made to deter thieves. A yellow strand came from Chatham, blue from Portsmouth and red from Devonport. To the seamen, this strand was the Rogue's Yarn.

The cook of a sailing ship could be either The Doctor or Old Slushy – possibly because of the quality of his food, while more recently a stores rating was Jack Dusty, from the dust of the stores.

While a bosun's mate was a Spithead Nightingale because of his call, or whistle, the chief petty officer of the Regulating Branch, the policemen or Master at Arms became a Jaunty, from the French gendarme. He could also be the Jossman while his petty officers were Crushers.

A leading seaman was known as a Killick while a signalman would be called Buntings, or perhaps bunting-tosser. Radio operators were Sparkers but when the electronic warfare operators came into being promotion was so rapid that the more traditional signalmen became not so much jealous as sardonic. The Electronic Branch were promoted so easily, they claimed, that they must buy their way up by collecting the Golliwogs from Robertson jam jars. From then on the Electronic Branch signallers were known as Golliwogs or Gollies.

On board the aircraft carriers, the Fleet Airarm ratings named the seamen as fish-heads, to get the retort of air-head or Wafus. On the same vessels the flight deck stokers who worked on the steam catapults were known as badgers. They wore brown and white striped jackets.

Even the Royal Navy ports had nicknames. Chatham was 'Up and at em', Portsmouth was Pompey and Devonport was Guzz –a place where the ships guzz in and out. Rosyth in Fife seems to have had no name but Inverkeithing was called Inverqueerthing, and not only by the navy.

But of all the nautical nicknames, probably the best known is the term Jack Tar which denotes a seaman. This is a very old name, coming from the days when the seaman's hands and clothing were covered in tar from the ship's ropes – and possibly from the even older days of tar covered ships in the Mediterranean. Tar was also used to waterproof the trousers of the men and was daubed on the long pigtails worn in the 17$^{th}$ and 18$^{th}$ centuries.

This was no affectation but acted as protection to the back of the neck from the slash of a cutlass in battle.

But the tar had some disadvantages as these lines from an 18th century shanty reveal:

*No indeed I'll wed no sailor, for they smell too much of tar,*
*You are ragged, you are sassy, get you gone you Jacky Tar!*
*You are ragged, you are sassy, get you gone you Jacky Tar!*

The fact that British seamen were ragged and therefore poor, continued into this century, where the street women of Lagos had their own little ditty of condemnation:

*Me no likee British sailor*
*Yankee sailor come ashore*
*Yankee sailor plenty monee*
*Me no jig-a-jig with you no more!*

If the British termed all Americans as Jonathans, the Americans could retaliate with the more truthful, and much more enduring, term of Limey.

Scurvy had been the curse of seamen for centuries. A terrible disease, which loosened the teeth, reopened old wounds, induced listlessness and frequently killed. In the 18th century it was realised that fresh fruit was anti-scorbutic and from there to a daily issue of limejuice was only a few decades. The fact that lemon juice, which was far more effective, had been suggested, was not generally realised.

Perhaps the mistake occurred because a lemon was called a lime in the Caribbean. Captain Cook was one of the earliest seamen to defeat scurvy, but he had to flog one of his men to encourage the others to eat the anti-scorbutic foods he issued. Both the Americans and the Australians have been credited for coining the term 'limejuicers', which was quickly shortened to 'limeys', and became used for a British person, nautical or not.

Some ships also tried rice as a preventative for scurvy. To the seamen, this was 'strike-me-blind'.

Centuries earlier British, but particularly English, seamen termed the Dutch as 'Butterboxes.' During the Dutch wars of the 1660s, this name was perpetuated in a boasting little couplet:

*The butterboxes brag no more*
*For now we have beaten you, o'er and o'er.*

Lower deck sailors had their own name for the Royal Navy. To them it was The Andrew. This comes from a noted press gang commander named Andrew Miller, who operated in the Portsmouth – Pompey – area. Miller pressed so many unwilling hands that they named the Andrew in his honour.

Other individuals have seen their name preserved by seamen. There was Charley Moore who ran a store in Malta, which had the slogan: 'Charley Moore – the Fair Thing'. From then, anything fair or honest became 'Charley Moore'.

At one time the galley funnel of a ship was termed a Charley Noble, after a Captain Noble who insisted on having his galley funnel sparkling bright at all times.

Then there is the Bloody Flag; a large red flag which ships of the Royal Navy wore when sailing into action. And the Red Duster, which British ships have worn since 1674, although then there was no Great Britain! While the English used St George's cross in the top corner, the Scots displayed the saltire of St Andrew. Until 1864 the Royal Navy also used the Red Ensign, but since then only merchant shipping has the right to sail under the Duster.

One thing remains common from all the nicknames; the irreverent attitude of the seamen to just about everything and everybody. There is neither false glory nor bombastic pride in their terms, no jingoism and no glamour. In only a few, deserved cases is there respect; the sea is certainly a great leveller.

No admirals are termed 'the Great' or 'the Conqueror', but neither are there any 'butchers'. Bully is the height of distaste and sometimes there is a hint of admiration in this. Seamen sink or sail on their own merits.

# 8 Women at Sea

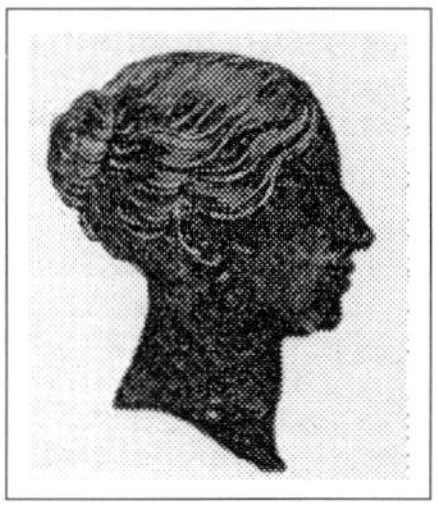

Many fine seamen have come from the villages of Fife in Scotland. Admiral Greig was one, Alexander Selkirk the privateer another and Captain Moodie of *Cutty Sark* a third. Yet not only the men of Fife ventured to sea.

In the kirkyard of Kilrenny, a seagull's call from the haven of Cellardyke, there is a weatherworn gravestone. Dated 17th December 1831, it marks the grave of one Thomas Watson who died at the age of 66. Carved into the grey stone are the bald words 'mariner, Cellardyke.' Yet that is to tell not a tenth of a seafaring saga which in itself hardly opens the door to a hitherto half-hidden world.

At the very end of the 18th century Thomas Watson was pressed into the Navy from his home village of Cellardyke. He was a fisherman and so should have carried a certificate of protection, but either he had forgotten it, or the Press took no notice.

At the same time as Watson was grabbed, so was Mary Buek his wife. Pressing a woman was highly unusual, but apparently Buek was a nurse and therefore would be useful at sea.

The couple stayed together through many years and many adventures. As Watson rose to be a bosun, Buek fell pregnant and in 1801, while HMS *Ardent* was cannonading Copenhagen, she gave birth to young Margaret. Both parents and their child were in *Victory* during the carnage at Trafalgar and if it was Hardy who gave Nelson his final kiss, it was Mary Buek from Cellardyke who prepared his body for embalming.

Such was the intensity of the battle that 85 years later Margaret could speak vividly of the action. Watson and Buek survived the war and returned to Cellardyke where they ran an alehouse for many years. But the true significance of this story lies not so much in the couple themselves – absorbing though their tale would be – but in the fact that there were women at sea.

'It's a man's life in the Navy'. 'Rum sodomy and the lash.' Two of the many clichés which tend to hide the number of women who did put to sea, and who shared in all the hardships and dangers of those arduous, cruel days.

Nobody doubts the toughness of the seamen, but the seawomen must have been a formidable crew too, and if Mary Buek was typical, they were supremely capable. The majority of wives are, given a decent man. But how many sea-wives were there?

The answer to that is unknown. As they were not officially on the strength of vessels, their numbers were not recorded, but there is a strong possibility that there were hundreds. As an example, when the frigate *Lapwing* was grounded near Beachy Head in 1801, there were around 40 women on board lending their strength at the ropes.

A 28-gun frigate was not a large vessel, with a crew, perhaps, of 200. And 40 women. This may have been an exceptional case, but it is possible that nearly every naval ship had some feminine presence.

At the Battle of the Nile John Nicol recorded that '...the women behaved as well as the men.' So well that some were wounded. One woman from Leith died of her wounds and another, from Edinburgh, gave birth to a son during the action.

Sometimes the women disguised themselves as men – although to achieve this on a crowded warship must have included some connivance from the hands. In 1807 HMS *Hazard* had a '...little female tar, Elizabeth Bowden' on board, but more honour goes to HMS *Queen Charlotte* in 1815. The captain of her maintop, a petty officer, was a negress. A prime seawoman who could not only reef, haul and steer but could supervise others doing the same. She had been at sea for upwards of eleven years!

In port, of course, there were many more.

It was not legal for a Royal Naval seaman to have a woman on board unless she was his wife. However the seaman had only to make a simple declaration that he was legally married for the woman to be allowed on board. This was in the days of pressed men, harsh conditions and no shore leave, as men allowed to go ashore were expected to desert.

Sometimes a Naval ship arriving in port would be welcomed by a fleet of bumboats, each containing two or more women and each woman willing to be a wife for the duration of the ship's stay. She would share her husband's meagre pay, share her body with him, and help mend and wash his clothes. And at the end of the ship's stay, she would be available for another vessel and another husband.

If the seaman had such a wife in every port, then there would be bumboat wives with a husband in many ships.

This was a union of necessity with neither glamour nor romance involved. Eighteen inches of hammock space to a man, eighteen to his wife, and then eighteen to another man and so on, man, wife and unattached all the squalid length of the lower deck.

Many women, of course, were genuine wives, faithful throughout all the difficulties of a long-distance marriage.

Some of the women who boarded the ship would have drink hidden beneath their voluminous skirts and although the officer of the watch would guess of its existence, he would not bother to search the carrier for a variety of reasons. Those women could be wild. It was said that the cockpit – a section of the lower deck – derived its name from the women who were stowed there. They fought like gamecocks.

Captain Richard Keates, an excellent seaman, used the women to his advantage for he rewarded good seamen with the presence of a female but withheld this privilege from the bad. Folklore of the 1840s claims that when one captain attempted to ban women completely, the crew mutinied. A sensible admiral sorted things out by sending a couple of hundred women on board — end of trouble.

Every warship carried a contingent of marines and sea soldiers such as these became involved in the attack on Pondicherry in the latter half of the $18^{th}$ century. In their ranks was one Hannah Snell of Worcester. During the battle, Snell was wounded in a delicate place, so to preserve her privacy and conceal her gender, she had to cut out the musket ball herself.

Snell survived her time at sea and retired to open a tavern in Uppington, still dressing in male clothes. Even this century, Wrens serving with the Royal Marines were known as Hannahs.

Britannia herself, of course, was a woman. She carried Poseidon's trident to show her sea power, but long before her time women had gone to sea.

One of the earliest and most formidable maritime cities ever, Carthage, dominated the western Mediterranean for centuries. It was Carthage which denied Greek seamen access to the Pillars of Melkarth and the western Ocean. It was Carthage that colonised the western half of the North African coastline and ventured into Spain. It was Carthage that pricked the pride of Rome and provoked that nascent empire into performing at sea.

And Carthage was founded by a female.

It all started with a power struggle in far-off Tyre, which resulted in Princess Elissa running for her life from her brother Pygmalion, King of Tyre. Pygmalion had murdered the high priest Archgabus, who was not only Elissa's husband but also her uncle.

Royal incest seems to have been tolerated in the ancient Levant.

Using her husband's fortune, Elissa purchased a whole fleet of ships – as the predominant Phoenician port, Tyre would have plenty – and pushed off to Cyprus. She had a number of followers with her, worried noblemen who were not in Pygmalion's camp and did as Elissa demanded. At Cyprus Elissa seduced a second high priest – she obviously had a penchant for religious men – and press-ganged 80 virgins, possibly the first recorded instance of that ignoble nautical tradition. But these unfortunate women were to become prostitutes for the glory of Astarte, not seawomen before the mast.

Astarte rather than Poseidon, but slavery none the less.

Heading west along the North African coast, Elissa located a handy promontory and asked the local Berber tribesmen if she could buy some land. 'Certainly' they agreed, 'as much as you can cover with an oxhide.'

'Perfect' replied the princess and, cutting a hide into thin strips, she surrounded a couple of acres of easily defended hillside. Enough to act as a base from which to expand. And from this beginning Carthage rose.

Strangely this story is not all fiction. Elissa was a real person, grandniece of the Biblical Jezebel, and she lived around 810 BC. Surely one of the most fascinating people of her time, but did a woman so obviously strong truthfully flee from her brother, or was this a planned Phoenician colony, away from the terrible power of Assyria?

By that time Spain had been discovered by seamen from Tyre and the North African coast would be known.

If the Dark Ages are well named with the limited illumination from surviving documentation, then the Middle Ages are not much better, at least where women played their part at sea. No doubt they were there, and no doubt they were as strong and skilful as their men, but little seems to have been written.

What is known, however, is fascinating.

There was Christiana MacRuairi, the Hebridean supporter of Robert Bruce, King of Scots. MacRuairi controlled Garmoran, a hugely scattered collection of lands and islands in the west. Nothing much is known of her, but the chronicler Fordun says of Bruce,

> *...through God's mercy, and with the help and by the power of Christiana of the Isles, a noble lady who wished him well, he returned to the earldom of Carrick.*

So few words hiding so much meaning! At that time Bruce was alone, hopeless, powerless. MacRuairi befriended him when his noble lords were afraid, she lent him ships and warriors and sent him away strengthened and no longer alone.

If by some twist of history, Bruce had married MacRuairi rather than the Anglo-Norman-Irish Elizabeth de Burgh, her loyalty and Gaelic spirit would surely have surged through the succeeding dynasty. Scotland might not have experienced the cataclysmic split between highland and lowland and centuries of torment may have been avoided.

Anyway, she deserved to be a queen.

And then there was Jean de Belleville. Like many people, de Belleville was jogging along quite happily minding her own affairs when fate intervened to throw her into turmoil. Again this was in the $14^{th}$ century, but this time her husband, a Breton nobleman, was beheaded for treason.

Whether he was a traitor or not is immaterial; much more important was the effect on his widow. Rushing to Nantes, where her man's head was on public display, de Belleville made her children swear to avenge his death, then she made a start herself. Whistling up some followers, de Belleville ran riot on land, then took to the sea with a fleet of ships with which she savaged the shipping of her enemies. With true Breton bravery, she was always first to board the enemy ship and surely saw her revenge when her son became Constable of France and victor of the battle of Duray in 1364.

Perhaps because it was outwith the established system, piracy was one area in which women made their mark. Clew Bay in Ireland was the home of the notorious Grace O'Malley who enjoyed more than one spouse, marrying first a wild O'Flaherty and then Richard 'of the iron' MacWilliam.

Both were hard men but Grace O'Malley, Captain Grace or Granuaile, was their equal. The O'Malley's of Clare were a maritime clan and Granuaile followed the tradition, and if legend claims that she tied up her ship to her toe by a clew, history records that she fought Sir Richard Bingham to a standstill.

For forty years she patrolled the seas between Spain and Ireland and although her crew was as truculent as any warrior Irish, they followed Granuaile with as much devotion as the Celts have always shown to their female leaders.

Folklore has Granuaile meeting England's Elizabeth at Greenwich, and a liking developing. That could well be true, for Elizabeth met that Scottish land pirate Scott of Buccleuch and treated him kindly. The English queen seemed to have a liking for boldness, legal or not.

Better known in the folklore of piracy are Betty Read and Anne Bonny. Read tried her hand at soldiering first, tramping to the tuck of a drum through Flanders mud before changing to prostitution and piracy.

Anne Bonny was the daughter of a County Cork lawyer, but not by his legal wife. She fell for the colourful pirate Captain Jack Rackham, but he was not game enough for her. When the Navy attacked his ship, Rackham fled below while Anne Bonny fought it out on deck.

Bonny was pregnant at the time and 'pleaded her belly' to escape the noose she deserved. Lacking this feminine escape clause, Rackham swung beneath the gallows tree. Bonny declared she '...was sorry to see him there, but if he had fought like a man, he need not have been hanged like a dog.'

Another woman pirate, on a far larger scale, was Mrs Ching, or more accurately, Ching Yih Saow. Like de Belleville, Mrs Ching was thrust into leadership by the death of her husband, Ching Yu.

It was 1807 when a China Sea gale sent Ching Yu to the bottom and left Mrs Ching in charge of 600 pirate junks. This was a larger fleet than that of the Royal

Navy and the largest carried thirty cannon. Mrs Ching put things in order, worked out a bureaucracy and a command structure and terrorised the coast of China. Blackmail and plunder was a way of life.

For five years Mrs Ching virtually controlled the coast and when she agreed to peace with the authorities she turned to smuggling instead. Not a woman for a quiet life, Mrs Ching.

Probably the seamen of the late 19th century had never heard of Mrs Ching, or Christiana MacRuairi, for they believed it unlucky to have a woman on board a ship. That might be classed as pure superstition, but in instance after instance it was proved true, and the unluckiest person was the wife of the captain.

In 1910 the ship *Swanhilda* was voyaging from Cardiff to the pacific coast of South America and the captain had brought his wife for her honeymoon.

On the sixth of May they were near Cape Horn in swirling mist when land was sighted dead ahead. Immediately the captain ordered *Swanhilda* onto the starboard tack, but he was too late. She ran aground at cape St Anthony. Because his wife was terrified, the captain joined her on the first lifeboat; the only one to capsize.

Nine seamen were drowned and when the captain and his wife were found later they were still embracing, but dead.

Again off Cape Horn two ships were passing close to each other when a huge wave swept them together. For an instant they rolled, side by side, both flanked by massive seas. Believing that his ship was going down, one captain lifted his wife and threw her onto the second ship, only to see the gap widen, then abruptly close. Caught between the two hulls, his wife was crushed to death.

There are many similar cases, but at other times the captain's wife was invaluable. Mrs Captain Poules of *John of Gaunt* was like a mother to her crew, tending the sick, giving maternal advice to those in need and darning the socks of the hard of foot. A true seawoman, she gave birth to a son while at sea and named him Thomas Mariner Poules.

And then there was Mrs Captain Hall of *Macduff*. The captain was out on a shooting trip while in California when a rattlesnake appeared. Jumping out of its road, the captain fell backward, onto a cactus plant. Probably hiding their amusement beneath a mask of concern, his officers brought Captain Hall back to his wife, who plucked the prickles from his bottom. It was quite a while before the captain could sit comfortably and poor Mrs Hall had to endure his bad temper.

But perhaps she kept a prickle or two as a reminder of the captain's misadventure. One thing is certain; at sea as on land, wives had the knack of controlling their men.

*The whaler* Diana *at Dundee. Judging from the bunting in the rigging, she is about to leave for the Arctic.* Courtesy of Central Library, Dundee.

# 9 Neptune, Nereids and a Master Carpenter

To the old shellbacks it would be an episode of high entertainment. To the uninitiated it would be a time of discomfort, humiliation and possibly fear. But that was the purpose of the ceremony; to amuse those sailormen who had already survived the ordeal of 'crossing the line.'

The Line was the Equator and those being initiated had never before ventured this far south.

On board HMS *Melville* in the 1830s. Petty Officer Bechervaise writes:

> *There were a great number on board the ship...who had never yet gone South of the Tropics; and so were to be initiated into...entering the dominion of Neptune.*

Preparations for the ceremony had begun even before the ship left England, with '...many a poor girl...' being deprived of some part of her wardrobe '...to adorn Aphrodite.'

Neptune and Aphrodite, dressed in long wigs and complete with crown and trident, ruled the ship that day so even the captain could not interfere.

'Neptune commands today' he said.

'The evening before we expected to cross the line, the lookout man reported ...a light ahead; presently a hoarse voice hailed 'ship ahoy' which being answered by the Captain, Neptune intimated his intention to visit the ship early next morning.'

To prepare for the honour, the ship furled most of her sails and readied a huge, eight-foot deep bath, into which the uninitiated, and so far unaware, hands pumped water. At ten in the morning Neptune, Aphrodite and their son Triton appeared in all their gaudy splendour. As Neptune, Bechervaise 'drunk a good health to the Tars of Great Britain.'

Those who had never crossed the Line were brought forward and although the officers could bribe their way to safety with bottles of rum, the hands lacked access to such luxuries and had to endure the pleasure of Neptune.

*...a bucket was filled with all the cleanings of the hen coops, pig sty's etc., and with it a due proportion of tar had been mixed, with a large paint brush dipped in the villainous compound, and his razor close to him, the barber stood waiting the signal.*

As the initiates opened their mouths to answer Neptune's first question, the paint brush went in. The same happened at the second question, and the third, until the beleaguered man was tipped into the deep bath.

For four hours the initiates were questioned and toppled, then followed an evening of festivities as Neptune was honoured.

This ceremony, or something very similar, was performed on most ships as they crossed the Line and as Neptune was the Roman God of the Sea, this could reveal the longstanding power of an ancient belief. Unfortunately, as Neptune was one of the more minor Roman deities and the Romans were pedestrian in their attitude to things nautical, it is more likely to reveal the strength of classical education in the collective mind of Western Europe.

Interestingly, there was also a belief that sailors who crossed the equator would become bald with scurvy. This had nothing to do with sea gods and everything to do with long voyages on a poor diet.

The sea peoples of the world have always felt compelled to grant the sea its own god, or if not that, at least a god whose moods and temperament reflect those of the sea. If the Romans had Neptune, then they had borrowed the concept from their more imaginative Greek neighbours. More imaginative and more nautical minded, for the coastal and insular Greeks were a race of mariners. Two of the most enduring of all legendary seamen were Greek: Odysseus and Jason, and both sailed in the cupped palm of their gods.

Poseidon was the Greek sea god and like his Roman successor he was depicted with a long beard and hair which flowed like the tide, while a three-pronged fishing trident was clutched in his fist. Overlordship of the sea had been granted to him by Fate.

Like other Greek gods, Poseidon was very human in both behaviour and desires; only his immortality and great powers set him apart.

A married god with seven children, Poseidon had a chariot drawn by creatures half horse, half serpent, and a court of sea spirits. He also had the ubiquitous Mediterranean dolphin. Loving the praise and good fellowship of mortals, Poseidon was easily hurt by the other gods of the Greek pantheon and once was even sentenced to slavery by Zeus, chief of all the gods.

As the central sea of half a hundred developing civilisations, the Mediterranean produced other sea deities, most of which are not well known.

Phoenicia, that enigmatic scatter of seaside city-states, had the infamous Baal, but it was the lesser god Yaam who was Prince of the Sea. In their inevitable conflict, Yaam came off second best, but perhaps this is an historical memory of the defeat of the Sea Peoples, the Philistines, in the $12^{th}$ century BC.

The Phoenicians also boasted the goddess Asherah of the Sea, whose unfortunate son died yearly in a form of harvest sacrifice.

In the Babylonian 'Poem of Creation' the sea god in the guise of the lady Tiamat again loses, this time to Marduk, the chosen leader of the gods.

Perhaps these people saw the sea as a threat to be challenged and defeated, rather than an ally to be coveted and caressed?

If that is so, then the Sumerians of southern Mesopotamia were less fearful. They had a goddess named Nammu, whose written symbol equated with 'sea' and who was also described as 'the mother who gave birth to heaven and earth.' So the sea was given priority, and out of the water came both the sky and the land.

None of these people had the imaginary scope and sea vision of the Greeks. As well as Poseidon the Greeks had the truthful, gentle Nereus, the original 'Old Man of the Sea' and Tethys.

Tethys was a sea goddess who married Oceanus, her brother and in this incestuous relationship she proved remarkably fertile. The three thousand offspring she produced became the waves of all the world's seas. One of these children was Doris, who married Nereus and their union was blessed with the Nereids, who rarely left their father's golden palace under the sea.

There was silver haired Thetis who danced on the shore; Kumu, the girl who played on the waves; Protho who smiled in the wake of sailing ships and offered pearls to the mariners; Amphirite, wife of Poseidon and Thetis, mother of Achilles. Others just spun and sang and watched the play of the dolphins.

Then there were the sinister Harpies, the Snatchers who personified the black side of the sea. Aello or Storm-Foot; Ocypete or Swift-Wing, and Celaena, the dark one who created the heavy cloud before the onset of a storm.

This trio of evil sisters was all-powerful and lived in the Ionian Sea. They would be seen as birds that clutched all they saw with their greedy, sharp claws.

Another threesome, the Graea or Old Women of the Sea, sisters of the horrendous Gorgon, lived beyond the sunset in a land of darkness and mist.

Perhaps native to that same land were the Celtic peoples who also had their quota of sea gods, and if there are no sea epics of the quality of the Odyssey, that may be due to the nature of the four seas surrounding the British Isles. No smiling Mediterranean here, but the rocks and squalls and mists of the north – and tales of Brendan the Navigator and other courageous men, which surely redress at least part of the balance.

Here, in this group of fertile islands, sea travel was common and the sea god Lir ruled. Lir or Llyr, the same god in different branches of a Celtic tongue.

While Lir ruled the sea, Nudd was the god of that land which lies under the waves: the Celtic underworld. And there was the Irish Bron, who sailed west to the Land of Beyond. But it was Manannan, son of Lir, who is daily and probably unknowingly, mentioned.

A magician with a fiery helmet, Manannan had a ship with neither sails nor ropes, which moved at his will. Seamen called him 'Lord of the Capes', the headlands of the west against which the Atlantic crashes in awesome fury, and they prayed to him for help.

His own kingdom, the Island of Man, in the middle of the Irish Sea, recalls Manannan and if this is a small kingdom for a god, it is also a remarkably beautiful one. And fortunate, for the Isle of Man has maintained her own parliament and laws for upward of a thousand years, unlike most of her larger neighbours. Manxmen are also renowned for their seafaring skill.

Sister of Lir was Branwen and she was a lover of many, free with her favours and as independent as the sea from where she came, or as Celtic womanhood has always been.

There seems to have been little fear of the Celtic sea gods, however fierce the Atlantic weather, for 'Evil does not come from the sea' is an old Scottish proverb and the land between high and low tide was a sanctuary, a place safe from persecution.

Yet few of these Scots are aware that their own Island of Arran was another home of Manannan and this despite the fact that the village of Lochranza once boasted more ship's masters than any other place in the west. Manannan seems to look after his own.

Not surprisingly, the Norse gods had a troublesome relationship with the sea. Thor himself, possibly the god closest to the heart of the fierce Viking warriors, was fated to fight forever against the giant sea monster whose coils encircle the earth and who creates all the storms of the sea. According to Norse mythology, only on the last day of the world with Thor kill this serpent of the Midgard and even then he will be killed himself.

There was also Aegir, 'Master of the Sea' whose golden palace was filled with the treasure of innumerable wrecks, and his wife Ran, the storm goddess. Norse seamen used to throw gold overboard to appease her on stormy days.

Outside Europe, the Chinese had Yu-ch'iang, who lived in the northern sea and had a dual personality, being both a wind god and a sea god.

As a god of the sea winds he had the body of a bird, the face of a man and two serpents coiled round his ears. As a sea god he had the body of a huge whale but with human hands and feet. Rather than swim, Yu-ch'iang was transported on a pair of dragons. It was Yu-ch'iang who created the terrible typhoon of the China seas, for when he became angry he mutated into a huge bird and his ascent from the sea produced massive waves.

If the Chinese mariners had sailed the vast sea to their east – and perhaps they did – they would have met another seafaring people. The people of the Gilbert Islands.

The Gilbertese came from the east in the distant past, sailing their double canoes across a thousand miles of ocean, and then a thousand more, seeing only the long Pacific swell stretching to the blue Pacific horizon. They were men and women of the sea and they knew the anger as well as the caress of the waves, perhaps like no other.

They knew of Tabakea, the great turtle who resided on the bed of the ocean and who supported on his massive shell the slender pinnacles which were topped by the islands the Gilbertese knew as home.

They also knew how Tabakea came to be down there, for it was one of their ancestors, Au-of-the-rising-sun who had forced Tabakea to remain on the sea bed. Au was the far-voyager, a famous lover, a fearful warrior, a hero indeed, yet it was to Tabakea that the islanders prayed for success at the fishing and for safe passage through the terrible reefs which protect so many of their islands from the sea.

A god in the shape of an ocean creature, a hero with the lustiest attributes of an adventurous people, and another ancestor named Nimanoa the Navigator. The Gilbertese had created a mythology from their own environment, and accepted that their world was intertwined with the sea.

On the distant shore of the Pacific, further east that even the Gilbertese could conceive and far to the north, the Haida people of what is now British Columbia and the Queen Charlotte Islands had their own unique culture, and their own unique mythology.

One of their tales tells of the Master Carpenter, a god-like being in a world where pine trees swept from the seas to a green forever. Master Carpenter had a disagreement with the South East Wind, who was so boisterous that Master Carpenter became annoyed and decided to calm him down. No easy task, to quieten an ocean wind.

However Master Carpenter tried his best. As the Southeast Wind lived in the south of the Queen Charlotte Islands, Master Carpenter needed a canoe but his boat building skills were not fully developed. So Greatest Fool (another deity from Haida mythology) revealed the secret of bent wedges and Master Carpenter built his canoe and paddled out to sea.

He challenged Southeast Wind but got no response until a sudden sea current thrust them together. Mixed with a tangle of seaweed was the hair of the Wind so Master Carpenter grabbed hold and hauled, until the Wind yelled lustily for help.

When the sky reddened, Master Carpenter realised that Red-Storm-Cloud had arrived, and then the wind strengthened as Taker-Off-Of-The-Tree-Tops came.

The tops of the tall pines swayed and fell around Master Carpenter's canoe, and only his magic saved him. A stronger wind, Pebble-Rattler, was joined by Maker-Of-The-Sea-Mist but still Master Carpenter fought, until Tidal-Wave capsized his canoe and the unequal combat ended.

The shamans of the Haida say that the Southeast Wind survived, and if the name of his mother, Tomorrow, is uttered, he will return with bad weather. That name is sacred to him.

These Haidan gods describe the folly, or perhaps the bravery, of man in challenging a Pacific storm. Yet further north still the Eskimos had their own sea goddess although her name changed from area to area. The most common is Sedna and the tales are similar. While escaping an unwelcome suitor, Sedna was thrown out of a boat by her father, but she clung to the gunwale in desperation.

Her father, however, was a cruel man and sliced off her fingers, one at a time, until she slipped through the depths to the sea bottom.

Down here Sedna keeps watch over all the sea creatures with her one eye. Married to a sea scorpion, black with the sins of man, Sedna punishes mankind for secrecy and can only be seen by the shamans of the Eskimos.

An ugly god, yet perhaps familiar to the persecuted, it is in the Mediterranean that the most foul of the sea god rituals occurred.

Before they attained the civilisation for which they are remembered, the Greeks used human sacrifice to pay their supposed debt to the sea god. In times of crisis an unfortunate man was taken to some public place and fed on barley bread, figs and cheese. After that he was ritually beaten with branches from specially selected trees, his cries being muffled by the tune of a flute. Then he was burned on a pyre and his ashes given to the sea.

This may well have been for the good of the community, but it is a reminder of the cruelty of man's ancient religions. In the Maldives, Ibn Batutah recorded the belief that an evil spirit sailed the sea, disguised as a ship full of burning lamps. When this thing came close, the Maldive Islanders left a young virgin in a temple beside the sea. By next morning the girl was no longer virgin and no longer alive. But the power of Islam came in the shape of a Berber, who rescued the last maiden chosen and drove back the evil spirit of ignorance.

To return to the Mediterranean; Venice, that city which depended entirely upon the sea and exists at the whim of the waves, had a different method of paying tribute. On Ascension Day the Doge, who ruled the city, was rowed into the Adriatic on a galley of incredible elaboration and there he ritually married the sea.

'I espouse you, oh sea' said the Doge 'in sign of your perpetual domination' and he threw an engraved wedding ring into the water.

This unlikely act gave Venice her title of Bride of the Sea and it was actually initiated by a Pope. In 1177 Pope Alexander III handed the Doge a ring from his own ginger to thank him for his naval help against his enemies.

So even the head of the Catholic Church had inside him a little awe of the power of the sea.

*Harpoonist on a Dundee whaler, c. 1900.* Courtesy of Central Library, Dundee.

# 10 The Greenlandmen

In the museum at Broughty Ferry, east of Dundee, there is an excellent section on Arctic whaling. Among the exhibits are a number of harpoons, including a couple which have been retrieved from the body of a whale. The contortions of these hefty lengths of iron not only illustrate the strength of the hunted animal, but also provide a microcosm of the entire whaling industry.

This was no sporting hunt for a trophy with which to adorn a wall. This was a serious business where death for the whale was the object, but death for the whaler was often the result.

Like most forms of hunting, whaling has almost always been with us. In the beginning the hunters killed those animals which were embayed, or which swam ashore in that mysterious confusion which affects whales. Then, as seamanship advanced and seamen became more daring, the hunt extended. To the Bay of Biscay; to the inshore waters of Western Europe, to the Gulf of St Lawrence and, finally, to the Arctic.

It was the Dutch who dominated the early Arctic whaling, sending hundreds of ships north, creating the prefabricated summer town of Smeerenberg in Spitzbergen and thinning the whale population so the hunters had to press further afield.

Whales were hunted for their oil, which was used in the jute industry, and in lamps and lights. They were hunted for whalebone or baleen, the fine mesh through which the whale siphons off its plankton food. This whalebone had a myriad uses; sieves and, hairnets, guards for shop windows, stays for fashionable ladies, carriage backs and bed bottoms. It seemed that the entire world revolved round whalebone and an average bowhead possessed about 700 pieces, some over four yards long.

But the whales too, valued this whalebone and sometimes fought to keep it.

By the end of the 18th century British whalers had elbowed into prominence and ships from London and Hull, Aberdeen and Dundee, Leith and Peterhead crunched through the northern ice.

Other seamen called them 'blubber boats' but they were well suited for their purpose. Wooden built with a double thickness everywhere except the treble thick bow and stern, they were additionally strengthened with internal oak beams and wood, or later iron, plates outside.

From these the whaleboats were launched to do battle with the whales.

Certain events became traditional in the whaler's calendar. On the last Sunday before the fleet sailed the ships were decorated with ribbons, the people of the port came on board and the local minister preached a sermon for the Greenlandmen, as the whalers were known.

On the day of sailing the whaler's girl would hand him a garland as both good luck charm and love token. The garland was of ribbon with one knot for each whale the ship would catch – but it was bad luck to count the knots until May evening. Married men, less fortunate, had to purchase their own ribbon from a speywife, who blessed them.

They were wild men, mostly young, and drink was their sin and their salvation.

The whales they sought were not defenceless. They fought with the flukes of their tail and one blow was enough to destroy a whaleboat. Men in broken or capsized boats had little chance of survival in the Arctic seas, even if they were rescued. Frostbite was nearly inevitable, followed by gangrene and the loss of fingers, toes, a limb or a life.

Take the case of the Dundee whaler *Chieftain* which had been hunting for bottlenosed whales in the Greenland Sea. The four whaling-boats were sent out but one of the unexpected fogs of the area descended. Cut off from their ship, the whaleboats made for Iceland, a full 200 miles away.

One of the four boats was never seen again. Two others were located by whalers but when the fourth boat was found there was only one member of the crew still alive. Frostbite had hit him hard; he lost both his legs.

In 1851 a boat's crew from Kirkcaldy was lost overnight. In the morning they were located, but all the men were frostbitten. Seven lost some of their toes; three died.

As an interesting alternative to smashing a boat, the whale could dive, and the whole boat might be dragged at speed a great distance from its mother ship. So the boats worked in teams. They attacked from the rear, thrust in the harpoon and backed off before the great flukes struck.

Occasionally a whale would drag a man under, or a line could loop around a careless arm or leg as the animal dived, resulting in mutilation or decapitation. Death could come in many forms in the Greenland fisheries.

So the men drank when they could, danced away their shore nights, acted like the 'wild southern boys' that the Shetlanders thought they were.

Although the whale is a mammal, the term 'fishery' referred to whale hunting.

There were two important aspects to the early fisheries. Firstly it was an excellent training ground for seamen; once they learned the rudiments of seamanship in the Arctic they could be pressed by the Navy. Secondly, and ultimately more important, was the commercial aspect.

Any profits made had to be balanced by the tragic losses. Every year men would die, or ships would go down. Some years were worse than others. In 1757 the British whaling fleet was caught in a storm at the fringe of the Greenland Sea and 17 ships were lost. In 1830 ice caught them crossing the Breaking-Up-Yard of Melville Bay; 19 ships were sunk.

Sometimes a whaleboat would be found with one or two or half a dozen dead men on board, staring sightlessly for a rescue, which never came. And in the 'coarse year' of 1854, there was a truly horrific sight.

It came floating toward the whaleship. An icefloe and a body of men enclosed within a wall of ice. Huddled men, survivors of some sorry ship, but men with the presence of mind to build a wall as some shelter from the cutting Arctic wind.

A boat was launched, landed on the floe and two men slithered toward the survivors. They were far gone for none lifted a hand in acknowledgement. Then the whaler men realised that there were no survivors; the men were long frozen and what had appeared to be a wall of ice was actually composed of iced corpses.

A full ship's crew must have landed as survivors on that icefloe and as they died the bodies were hauled to the side and added, one corpse on top of another, to the wall. Seventy men were dead there, amidst the utter desolation of the north.

It was a fate that awaited every Greenlandman and they knew it. But there was always the rum.

Alcohol added to the gaiety of departure when they left their homeports with brave ribbons dancing from their rigging and half the crew drunk and incapable. Alcohol helped the hilarity of Mayday, when Neptune visited the ship to indoctrinate the First Voyagers.

But not all whalemen drank. There was 'Coffee Tam' Robertson of Peterhead, a teetotaller and an excellent captain.

There was singing and dancing too. A dance was often held on board the day before sailing with a melodeon blasting out to hide the tears of fearful wives who clung to the men they might never see again. Songs like 'Bonnie Ship the Diamond' were sung in celebration of one ship's tremendous catches when the crew made money and their wives could pay the rent and feed the bairns without fear.

Few mentioned that *Diamond* was sunk on a later voyage.

'Bonnie Laddie, Hielan Laddie' was another whaling song, sung as the boats' crews towed the whale from the killing site to the mothership. This could be a long haul, hour after hour with the dead weight dragging back on the boat and the constant threat of snow or fog.

Men lived with the ice and in fear of the ice. Sometimes the ice spoke directly to them. If the sea was flat and the air crisp, there was often a weird sound on the east side of Melville Bay. To the seamen, this could be the cry of the lost whalingmen, or the wail of the ice itself. Captain William Barron described it as '...a strange phenomenon, resembling a very weird whistling in a high note,' This sound was only heard at sea level, from a ship's boat. 'On the deck it seldom can be heard.'

Then there was the 'ice blink,' this was the Greenland-man's term for the reflection of light from the ice on the sky. When the sky was dark ahead, that showed that there was clear water called a 'water sky'; but if the sky was white, or pink, there would be ice. That was an 'ice sky'.

Even the smell of ice was distinctive to the whaleman. It was a Cape Horn clipper who said; 'You could smell ice ahead in the Southern Ocean well in advance, whereas the bergs on the Grand Banks give no warning.'

In October 1835 neither lore nor smell nor sound helped the Arctic seaman when the ice closed round the fleet in Baffin Bay. As was common in merchant ships, supplies were both poor in quality and limited in quantity and when the captain of *Middleton* rationed food, the crew planned a mutiny.

William Elder, the mate of *Viewforth,* whose ship was also helpless in the ice, watched the mounting trouble with some unease. He expected either a deputation or a demand for food from *Middleton*, and wrote, '... it will end in nothing but man to man for his dear life.'

Ice pressure continued and snuffed out the mutiny as *Middleton* was sunk; her crew scattered to others of the fleet. *Dordon* was next; lifting

> *three or four feet out of the water. If you had heard the crackling and cringing of the ship it would make the very flesh creep along your back,*

That was not the end; it took five days for *Dordon* to sink as ice punctured her hull and her crew punctured the spirit stock. A gaggle of drunken seamen set a fire for warmth and *Dordon* burned nicely.

Five ships remained trapped that December, with ice below decks, ice on the occupied beds and the crews playing cards, yarning and trying not to think about death in the ice. When food ran low men slithered and cursed over to the wrecked ships for more. At least two of these men died of frostbite.

Scurvy arrived in January, weakening the men and killing some so the master of *Jane* wrote 'It truly is a wretched miserable life, prolonged for what?'

*Jane* was one of the luckier ships; along with *Viewforth* she eased from her prison that same month and staggered to Stromness. There were only seven fit men on *Viewforth* but *Jane* had a full crew.

That left three ships still beset, and while two of them, *Abram* and *Lady Jane* sailed home safely, the last, *William Tore* was never seen again. The ice had sunk her and the entire crew died, despite the efforts of the local Eskimos.

And there were other hazards for the Greenlandmen. The back end of the $18^{th}$ century was a bad time in the north, for not only was there a war with the French, but also a rebellion in the American colonies.

The American privateers were a daring bunch who thoroughly enjoyed biting the hand that taxed them. When they raised their flag of jaunty defiance they were soon joined by France, Spain and eventually nearly all maritime Europe, eager to puncture the smug arrogance of Britain.

That war ended, soon to be replaced by the longer and more dangerous French Revolutionary War. To the whalers it meant the same; privateers, pressgangs, privation. In 1797 *Robert* of Peterhead was cheekily attacked off her homeport and only saved by the shore batteries. The Leith whaler *Simon* was particularly unlucky. In 1806 she was caught in a storm and driven ashore at Houten Head. Refloated, she sailed again, only to be recaptured and burned by the French *Le Guerriere.* Privateers took *William* that same year and although the Navy rescued her, many of her crew were pressed.

In 1813 *Eliza Swan* of Montrose was captured by the heavy American frigate *President* and had to pay to be released, so it was little wonder that many whalers carried cannon, sailed in convoy and used a protection certificate against impressment. Often these certificates were ignored and the whalers fought the Navy with flensing knives, or left their ship miles from their home port.

Perhaps it was this very self-reliance which gave British whalers the edge over American competition. When the 1812 war broke out, many British whalers carried Letters of Marque and fell on the Americans, either out of patriotism or commercial rivalry.

This private enterprise was particularly effective in the Pacific where both nations hunted, and the United States government sent USS *Essex* to retaliate. She did this in style, and although the Royal Navy eventually took *Essex*, her depredations virtually ended British whaling in that ocean.

The Americans sailed from Nantucket or New Bedford to hunt the sperm whale.

Herman Melville immortalised these years-long voyages in his 'Moby Dick' but there was as much truth as fiction in his words. In November 1820 the Nantucket ship *Essex* was sunk by a great sperm whale and the same happened to *Ann Alexander* in 1851.

As the $19^{th}$ century wore on, whaling continued to produce colourful personalities. There was Charles Yule who was a captain in the timber trade when he ran the Danish blockade of Prussia. With the timber, he built *Esquimaux*, sailed her to Canada and Russia and in 1866 strengthened her for the whaling.

'By the pipes of war!' Yule swore and at the start of every voyage he addressed his crew, 'Men, I am here to do my duty and I am going to see that you are helped to do yours.'

This adventurous man last commanded *Esquimaux* in 1879 and in 1883 retired to become Harbourmaster of Dundee.

However hard the life, the Greenlandmen returned year after year to the north. For some it was the only occupation they knew but others actually revelled in Arctic conditions. Often they brought an element of fun onto the ice. Rival crews of whalers slipped, skidded and swore as they played soccer with footballs of sealskin, although the team from *Victory* experienced some football hooliganism when a polar bear attacked the players.

All this was extra to the main purpose of the Greenlandmen, the hunting of whales. From the second the whaling ship entered hunting waters, the men waited for the call:

'Thar she blows!'

# 11 Pressing Jack

There was consternation in Portpatrick that December morning in 1813. Britain was at war with both France and America and a strange vessel was hovering offshore.

It was not unknown for American raiders to pounce on places like Portpatrick. During the last American war Dunbar had duelled with Captain Fall while the notorious John Paul Jones had probed both the Solway and the Forth.

Drums drew the Dumfries militia from domesticity to their duty, the Collector of Customs galloped to Greenock to notify the Navy and the people of Portpatrick collected their courage and what weapons they could find to fight off any landing party.

Dawn would increase the tension; the ship with guns grinning through open ports and the population, backed by the brightly uniformed militia, hoping they would not have to fight, but determined to resist.

As the light strengthened, the ensign of the menacing warship could be seen; not a circle of stars with horizontal stripes but the interwoven crosses of the Union. As the British warship launched a longboat, the Portpatrick men broke and bolted for safety.

Facing an enemy was bad enough but a landing by the Royal Navy meant the one thing that nobody wanted to risk.

The Press. The hated pressgang with its cutlasses and cudgels, its burly petty Officers and sadistic lieutenants.

When the longboat landed it was the women who met the landing party and, in a confused melee of shrewd blows and high abuse, sent them scurrying back to sea.

Although the power of the press probably peaked during the Napoleonic Wars, the institution was far older. In 1216 King John of England set the trend by seizing the seamen from all the ships lying off English ports. From that time on, mariners were fair game for the king's service.

In 1667, at the height of the Dutch Wars, an English frigate attempted to press Scottish seaman at Leith. Only the intervention of a troop of Scottish cavalry saved the seamen.

The press was seen less in peacetime. Then the captain of a king's ship encouraged volunteers from the adventurous, foolish or unemployed, but in time of war any seaman was liable to be summarily recruited into the Navy. Here he found conditions much less comfortable than in the merchant service.

Discipline was harsh, from 'starting' with rope ends or rattan canes, to flogging round the fleet or death by hanging. Food was coarse and frequently near inedible. Commissions sometimes lasted years, with leave non-existent. Death was common, more by disease than by enemy action, and the pay was terrible.

A merchant seaman would never be rich, but he could make a reasonable living, while the wages of a naval seaman had not altered since the days of the Stuarts. Recruiters stressed the two compensations of naval life: rum and the possibility of prize money.

The term 'press' was a shortened version of The Impress Service, which was the branch of the Navy responsible for gathering the requisite number of seamen for the fleet. Every port in the country was under the shadow of this service, with the more important having a captain in charge, the smaller a lieutenant. At the end of the 18th century there were 29 captains and 60 lieutenants on this duty, and if they were professional seamen they must have been embittered by this downturn in their careers.

It was these officers who led most of the pressgangs which scoured the haunts of seamen and earned the reputation so well remembered in sealore. These were the gangs of billy-club carrying ruffians who knocked poor tarry Jack on the head and carried him into the foulness of a holding ship until he could be placed on a seagoing vessel. These were the monsters that cut the waistbands of possible runaways so they could not escape without losing both their balance and their dignity as their trousers slipped round their ankles.

These gangsters were not seamen, who were far too valuable for such degrading work, but the scruffs and bullies of the dockside taverns. As well as the coastal areas, the gangs hunted inland for likely victims. Any man in trousers was suspect, for landsmen wore breeches. Any man who appeared unused to wearing shoes, for seamen were habitually barefoot. Any man with a nautical bearing, or who could not prove he did not belong to the sea, could be pressed.

Or frequently, anybody else who took the gang's fancy.

Often the press were informed of the whereabouts of a possible seaman, for the £1 reward was easy money. Women were particularly useful here. To entice a sex-starved seaman then get him drunk, use him, rob him and whistle up the press was a good night's work for some of the harpies who hovered around the docks.

On the other hand, some gangs could be bought off, and some people were immune. Gentlemen could not be pressed and, theoretically, neither could men carrying a 'protection.' This was a document signed by a local dignitary that named the carrier and informed the reader that he was '...hereby required and directed not to impress...' the bearer, unless '...the protection should be found about any other's person...' in which case impressment was ordered.

As can be expected, there was a thriving black market in these documents, forgeries were common and there was never a guarantee that the ogres of the press would honour a protection anyway.

During the construction of the Bell Rock lighthouse off the mouth off the Forth the workers had special medals that warned off the press. As the lighthouse was in itself a protection for all seamen, it was surely in the Navy's best interests to honour these medals.

Many maritime areas had specially constructed hidey-holes for vanishing seamen. False doors, double-bottomed chests, spaces behind the chimneybreast, or in the more rural areas, hollow haystacks and cavities in a midden heap or peat stack.

The press, however, did not always have things their own way. The people of a port could resist, with the women particularly active in defending their men from a prolonged period of misery.

In 1776 there were many deaths in Liverpool as press gangs clashed with reluctant seamen and their families. In the same city in 1778 pressed men were being rescued by bands of armed seamen who acted, according to the mayor, in a 'riotous and unlawful manner.' In London in 1790 a press gang took a coachmaker and was attacked by his colleagues. The gang was defeated, the lieutenant in charge being badly injured. Pressed men on *Tasker* in 1755 mutinied, ran the ship aground and escaped.

For all the organisation of The Impress Service, by far the majority of seamen pressed were actually taken at sea. Homecoming merchant shipping was the main target of the Navy and it was deeply ironic that the merchant seaman's time of most anxiety came while he was actually in sight of a homeport.

As an example, at the beginning of 1793, the press took literally thousands of seamen from the Thames. Many of these men would be native Londoners with their homes only a seagull's call away. Imagine the heartache of a wife or a girlfriend who actually witnessed her man being lifted and transported aboard a man of war. No wonder there was no love for the gangs.

The approaches to London, Bristol or any major port were constantly watched by the Navy, who had the right to remove the wretched seamen from merchant ships. The law stated that sufficient hands should be left aboard to navigate the ship into port, but often only the master, mate and a ship's boy were left aboard. Again, there were many attempts to construct hiding places on board these vessels, but as the boarding officers were experienced seamen, they probably knew all the tricks. And once located, all were grist to the ever-demanding mill of the Navy. Foreign seamen, after two years in a British ship, could be pressed. Foreign seamen with a British wife could be pressed. Even foreign seamen captured in battle could be pressed.

This free ranging concept of Britishness was one reason for the 1812 war with America. But British seamen also resented being pressed.

Robert Hay, taken in London in 1811 by '...six or eight ruffians who I immediately dreaded and soon found to be a press gang...' was brought to an examining officer, who asked:

'Are you willing to join the King's Service?'

'No sir.'

'Why?'

'Because I get much better wages in the merchant service and should I be unable to agree with the Captain I am at liberty to leave him at the end of the voyage.'

Dragged below, Hay was 'thrust down among five or six score of miserable beings who, like myself, had been kidnapped.'

William Richardson, pressed in Calcutta slightly earlier had similar thoughts. '...Shipwreck and the loss of all our clothes is distressing enough, but to be pressed into the bargain is really shocking; and I began to despond even to tears at my hard fate.'

Perhaps it was hard fate, but the naval authorities did what they could to obtain willing recruits. They had their own slogan 'better one volunteer than three pressed men' and attempted to persuade even those men dragged on board to volunteer.

There were recruiting parties in many dockside taverns, waiting to press the king's fatal shilling into an unwary palm. Or if that failed, to slip the coin into a mug of ale. So glass bottomed tankards came into fashion, enabling the drinker to watch for the treacherous gleam of silver among his dark dregs.

Then there was the bounty, known as 'conduct money' that was presented to every volunteer. Add that to the two months advance of pay and the prospect of naval employment suddenly seemed less grim. That was until the volunteer boarded his ship and discovered that the advance money would be quickly spent in paying for his hammock, his blanket and his cold weather clothing.

But there was always the rum. That was genuine. A tot of grog at noon each day; the holy oil which anointed the naval seaman's marriage with the service.

When the government ordered fixed quotas of seamen to be raised from every port, the maritime towns gladly unloaded their unwanted, their cripples and their criminals.

The government applied more pressure and that same year placed a six-week embargo on merchant shipping, until 20,000 men were raised.

The struggle between the nation's desperate need for seamen and the individual's desire for a decent life continued throughout the Napoleonic Wars. In 1804 a French squadron pounced on a convoy of 27 British merchantmen homeward bound from Canton. Of the British, fifteen were Indiamen, commanded by Captain Nathaniel Dance in *Earl Camden* while the French had one battleship, three frigates and one armed brig.

Signalling navy-style, Dance led *Earl Camden, Ganges* and *Royal George* directly at the French, firing every gun that could bear until the French ran. Even then the merchantmen pursued, saving the convoy.

Heroes all, they arrived in England where Dance was rewarded by the East India Company. At the same time the Navy quietly pressed the crews. After a six months voyage, these seamen had not been permitted a single day at home before they were back at sea.

The peace of 1815 saw the end of government pressgangs although the conscription of both 20th century world wars was a similar, if more efficient, concept. Unofficially, seamen remained in danger from a parasitical breed of landsmen known as crimps.

'These evil creatures' as R.L. Stevenson termed them, infested the dockside areas of many ports, and it was their function in life to obtain seamen for whichever merchant ship was short-handed. Robbing Peter to pay Paul was quite common.

They were totally unscrupulous, using bribery or drugged drinks to entice a seaman into their malevolent talons. Failing that, there were more direct methods, such as sandbags, blackjacks or the simple swing of a cudgel.

During the latter decades of the 19th and the early years of the 20th century, the Pacific coast of America seemed to attract the worst of these people. San Francisco, Seattle, Tacoma, Portland all had their infamous crimps. They became so influential that they virtually controlled the labour market for shipping, and captains were forced to pay blood money for each seaman he needed.

Sometimes blood money was an appropriate term, for corpses could be damped on board in the guise of men comatose with drink.

As soon as an inward bound ship slipped into harbour the crimps would meet it, rowing out with bottle shaped bribes and insincere smiles.

Rather than submit to this blackmail, Captain Batchelor of the full rigged *Cedarbank* sailed from Hong Kong with only half his compliment of seamen. In Portland, Oregon the crimps clustered round, demanding £60 for each seamen they supplied. In reply Batchelor had *Cedarbank*'s anvil dropped into one of their boats.

Even so, two of his crew were lured ashore and another two arrested on a false charge. Perhaps anger replaced his judgement as Batchelor left the ship to take personal vengeance on the crimp concerned.

Arrested for attempted murder, Batchelor left orders for his mate to shoot any crimp who boarded *Cedarbank*. And when the court discovered that the local sheriff was brother to the injured crimp, the charge of attempted murder was dropped. After one month in jail, Batchelor took *Cedarbank* out to sea. When a small boat hailed him, ordering a return to port, Batchelor continued to sail.

Not surprising, really.

One of the most feared of these predators was a certain Shanghai Brown. To shanghai a seaman was to either knock him out or drug him, then ship the unconscious man on a long voyage, but in 1896 Brown ran foul of the brassbounders of the ship *Springburn*.

Brassbounders were the ship's apprentices and they could be as wild as any young men. *Springburn*'s brassbounders were especially noted for their spirit and that year they captured Shanghai Brown and sent him on a voyage round Cape Horn. In the depths of winter.

A fitting fate for a crimp.

But the crimps, like the pressgang, are gone. A seaman in Liverpool or Leith, 'frisco or Falmouth, is safe from either the batter of a bosun's bludgeon or the sandbag of a hired bully. There are no longer harbourside pubs boasting a 'hole in the wall' from which to watch for an approaching naval party, nor are the women of Portpatrick or Portsmouth waiting to fight for their men.

And in that respect the good old days are better gone.

# 12 The Survivors

When the French ketch *J.B. Charcot* put into Tristan da Cunha in early 1908 the crew was greeted by a tall man, broad shouldered and dignified. This was Andreas Ripetto and once he had been a professional seaman. Raymond Du Batty, captain of the ketch, was curious about this man and asked how he came to Tristan. The answer was simple.

Ripetto was Genoese and with a fellow shipmate, Gaetano Landrello had been shipwrecked. Ripetto decided to settle here, 'not because it was the most attractive spot in the world, but because it was dry land and could not well be wrecked...Never again, ' Ripetto claimed '...would he put foot upon the deck of a vessel after one deliverance from death by drowning!'

Ripetto was not the first to be wrecked on Tristan, and others also decided to settle on this remote Atlantic island. In 1820 *Sarah* was lost here and three survivors remained on Tristan. Next year *Blendon Hall* struck nearby Inaccessible Island and those who remained of the crew were brought to Tristan by an ex-sailor named Glass.

At one time there had been a garrison here, probably with the object of denying the island to the French, for Bonaparte was then detained at St Helena a mere thousand miles or so to the north. Glass had remained when the rest of the garrison departed.

Other characters who were thrown upon the rocky shore by fate or storm included a seaman named Cotton who had guarded Bonaparte for three years, a man named Swain who had caught Nelson as he fell at Trafalgar and one Thomas Currie who declared the island a 'Sovereign Power' with himself as king. At that time Tristan had a population of precisely three.

There are probably as many tales of survival at sea as there are of shipwreck, and most people will have some image in their mind of half a dozen bedraggled survivors sitting in a lifeboat as their ship sinks slowly behind them.

One of the most famous, and deservedly most written about, survivors was the young Poon Lim. He was a steward aboard the British ship *Benlomond IV* that was sailing in the South Atlantic in November 1942 when a U-boat torpedoed her.

In the confusion and carnage, Poon Lim managed to scramble onto a life raft. He remained there, in the glaring sun of the tropics, in seas infested with sharks and with no sign of rescue. Days passed, then weeks, stretching to months and Poon Lim remained on his raft, not only alive but also aware and healthy.

It was 133 days before he was picked up, te sole survivor of *Benlomond IV.* He was transferred to a Brazilian hospital where he was examined, bedded down and kept, but only for a couple of weeks. Then he was fit to return to Britain.

When King George VI awarded him the BEM it was for his 'exceptional courage, fortitude and resource' but when Poon Lim attempted to join the US Navy he was refused because he had flat feet. In 1983 he retired as Chief Steward in the United States Line – a tremendous survivor.

There are no typical survivors; every person who lives through a shipwreck has a unique story to tell – of courage, endurance, luck, skill or a combination of some or all of these. Having said that, there are some accounts that incorporate many factors common to most wreck and survival stories. Storms, hidden rocks, misfortune, bravery, and the lone boat in a vast ocean.

It was six in the evening of Sunday 21st July 1889 when the barque *Mallsgate,* on passage from New South Wales to San Francisco, ran aground on Middleton Rock. Huge breakers thundered over the ship and washed away all the loose items on deck. Aloft there was chaos as spars split and fell in a tangled mess of ropes and wood.

In this horror somebody shouted 'She's filling!' and Captain McAdam had the mainmast chopped down to try and stabilise the ship until the boats were lowered. It is hard to imagine the confusion: the heeling ship, the surging grey and white sea; the yelling men as the axes hacked at the mast.

Darkness added to the nightmare and the cargo of coal had rumbled free, spilling black and evil below decks. The lifeboat and pinnace were launched but although stores and water had been placed in the lifeboat, the pinnace, 21 feet long and with nine men on board, had only two gallons of water, one pound of biscuit and one tin of fish.

With Captain McAdam in charge, the second and third mate, the carpenter, two apprentices and three seamen, the pinnace had a top-heavy command structure and as she swung clear of *Mallsgate,* she touched either the reef or the ship and her rudder snapped.

Mischance upon disaster but a jury rudder was contrived, in the dark and with a rising wind, and when an attempt by the lifeboat to throw out a towrope failed, the pinnace was alone with the sea.

Throughout that violent night the crew of the pinnace bailed for their lives but hope was kindled when they raised a storm sail at dawn. There was no sign of the lifeboat, no sign of land, only the foam crested waves, as the pinnace lay hove-to for a day and a night. When the weather eased to a mere gale a double reefed mainsail was set and McAdam steered for Australia.

Already it was Tuesday night and the water was nearly finished. The men were tired but the pinnace made a little progress and McAdam was cheerful but only until Thursday when worsening weather forced them to take in the mainsail, rehoist the storm jib and heave to.

That was the worst night so far as a high north-westerly wind pounded the hungry, thirsty, flagging men. Two became unconscious and those bailing were so weak they struggled to lift the full bailers One man died. Conditions deteriorated. By Friday afternoon even the storm jib had to be reefed and as darkness fell two waves smashed into the pinnace so she filled with water.

'Bail out boys!' the captain croaked and, using everything that came to hand, they did so. All longed for their single glass of water at dusk but for one man it was not enough; he drank seawater and died that night. Rather than pity, his shipmates were glad he had escaped this torment. Some wished to join him soon.

By Saturday night only four had the strength to continue but next day they sighted land.

This was Moreton Island, north-east of Brisbane, but when McAdam attempted to thrust through the south passage to clearer water, he was frustrated by high seas. There were breakers here, each capable of swamping or capsizing the pinnace with her weak crew.

A sudden surge of hope as a steamer was seen, and a last terrible effort was made. The four fittest: Mcadam, the second mate, the carpenter and an apprentice tried to row toward the steamer but were too weak. Skin peeled from salt-water-softened hands.

They were so close to safety and yet were dying fast. As a last desperate fling they tied a handkerchief to an oar and thrust it upright. Perhaps that tiny flutter was noticed because the steamer stopped and then, in what must have been a sickening moment, it moved off again.

Now there was no hope and no water; the high breakers on Moreton Island prevented a landing and the survivors must have expected to die that night.

But another dawn came and they were still clinging to life. An inshore current had grasped them, slid them into the land and they came ashore near Cape Moreton. Locating a waterhole, they drank themselves full. After that things became easier; a local lighthouse signalled for help and a steamer carried them to Brisbane where the crew of the lifeboat met them.

If the resourcefulness and determination of the captain had kept the crew of the pinnace alive, why had the hands made such a poor showing? It is quite likely that low quality food had weakened them. British ships were notorious for short rations and bad food, but as the years passed and the quality of food improved, so the stamina of the ratings and therefore their ability to survive increased.

During the Second World War there were numerous occasions where seamen survived after their ships were torpedoed.

On April 20$^{th}$ 1942 SS *Harpagon* was torpedoed while with a New York bound convoy. Although *Harpagon* went down in a few minutes, many of her crew leaped free, including Chief Engineer Lumsden and Second Officer Perkins. Both shared a lifeboat with another survivor, and helped hail five more men from the sea. There were other rafts nearby, mainly damaged, and Lumsden located drinking water and food. For thirty-four days they survived, until rescued by a Captain Capurso, who had himself survived shipwreck.

The second example involves Captain George Robinson's ship which was sunk in the North Atlantic. He and a Lewisman named Paterson were two of only four survivors. For four weeks they sailed a ship's boat before a passing ship rescued them. Of the four, only Paterson did not need help to climb into the rescue ship and four days later Paterson was fit to return to sea.

Malcolm Morrison was another case entirely. In November 1939 he was a 16 year-old deckboy in *Arlington Castle* when she was torpedoed in the North Atlantic. Eventually finding a lifeboat, Morrison realised that he was not only the youngest of the seven men on board but also the most experienced. As the others were cooks or stewards, they could not row and neither did they know anything about the sails.

Without Morrison they would have been helpless.

Morrison took the helm and for the next six days he directed the boat virtually without sleep or help, until they made landfall in South Uist. Then, according to the story, Morrison lifted an oar, balanced it on one shoulder and walked home.

Strangely, the main facts are true. Morrison was only 18 when *Arlington Castle* was sunk, and he did clamber aboard a lifeboat, which held two deckboys, a cook, an engineer and a fireman. As he sat there the U-boat slid underneath them 'so close' said Morrison 'I could have touched the periscope.'

There was water in the lifeboat, and some bully beef, which Morrison threw in the sea as the salt content, would increase their thirst. There were flares, but nobody saw their angry glitter in the sky, or perhaps nobody could spare the attention to come. After six days a Norwegian tanker rescued them. Morrison, who was the only man present with any sea knowledge, had sailed three hundred miles and was headed for the English Channel.

Like Paterson, Morrison was from Lewis.

The ordeal of some survivors was less prolonged, but had dangers more subtle than drowning or exposure.

In 1805 the French battleship *Achille* sailed to challenge the Royal Navy. Among the crew was a young gunner, and as his new wife could not bear to be without him, she had stowed away disguised as a seaman.

Throughout the long voyage to the Caribbean and back, husband and wife remained together but were separated as the opposing fleets closed off Cape Trafalgar.

When the fighting began the wife, Jeanette remained in the orlop, one of the safest places on board, but hideous with the sights and sounds of wounded men.

Only when *Achille* was set ablaze and the deck above her on fire did Jeanette leave the orlop. Probably she was forced into action when one of the deck guns smashed through the fire-weakened timbers. To an experienced man, life on a burning ship would be frightening; to a young woman searching for her husband, it must have been something out of a nightmare.

Screams and death, the solid ship smoking, blazing, timbers crackling, oaths and orders half heard through the terrible noise; people dimly seen in the acrid smoke and the prospect of death or injury at any time.

Scrambling through a gunroom port, Jeanette perched on the rudder chains, searched frantically for her man, but could not see him. The fire had reached the rudder and molten lead had seeped down, dripped onto her clothes so they began to smoulder. The fire spread and she could not beat it out.

In pain and panic, Jeanette tore off her burning clothes and leaped into the sea. There were other survivors amidst the pieces of broken ship and Jeanette swam to a floating spar. The French seaman already in possession kicked at her and bit her when she came too close and Jeanette backed away.

Another spar drifted past and Jeanette took hold, keeping her chin above the lapping waves as *Achille* flared and smoked close by.

There were many heads in the water, among the casks, spars and unidentified pieces of timber. A black pig swam by and then came a ship's boat, smartly manned with seamen lifting survivors out of the water.

Thankfully, Jeanette let herself be rescued, careless that her rescuers were British, careless that she was stark naked.

To the British seamen she must have been a rare sight, something to sweeten an exhausting day and they cared for her well, clothed her in a seaman's jacket and trousers and sent her, with other prisoners, to *Revenge*.

There was no malice between the seamen on either side; those British who were cast ashore in Spain were equally well treated.

It was perhaps natural that an attractive young Frenchwoman should become a favourite aboard a British ship. Officers competed for Jeanette's attention, gave her clothes and told her that her husband was alive and well, and a fellow prisoner.

Perhaps Jeanette was lucky, if anybody in a shipwreck can be considered so, but life at sea can be grim, and not everybody is willing to help the unfortunate.

In 1911 the Maritime Convention Act, Section 6, declared that the Master of a British ship who does not '...render assistance to every person who is found at sea in danger of being lost' is guilty of a misdemeanour. The vast majority of British ships' masters need no such official order to do something which is natural to them. But not all seafarers have the same compassion.

Sixty years after the Act, *City of Edinburgh* was sailing in eastern waters when she came across MV *Lira,* ablaze and in distress. Twenty-five men were rescued, comprising Filipinos, Burmese, Indonesians and Maldive Islanders. On that same voyage, *City of Edinburgh* met a small boat holding nine Vietnamese.

These people had joined the exodus of boat people and were being rescued a second time. A South Korean vessel had already helped them; only to put them back on their unseaworthy vessel when their nationality became known.

Rescuing Vietnamese fugitives was too much trouble. Sometimes the boatpeople had to make great efforts to fend for themselves.

At the end of July 1980 a group of families from the Saigon area decided that conditions at home were untenable so they would become refugees. By persuasion and probably a little bribery, the refugees obtained a landing craft that was under repair in Saigon naval dockyard. Thirty men filed on board, twenty-five women, one heavily pregnant, and seventeen children.

It is possible that they underestimated the length of their proposed journey, or they thought that the fuel supply of the landing craft would last longer. After three days the fuel was finished. As the landing craft was not designed for sustained voyaging but for a short ship to shore journey, this was hardly surprising. When a current pulled them back toward Vietnam, the refugees frantically hoisted an old parachute as a makeshift sail.

Although this halted their drift toward the land, they were barely making progress and then a flotilla of fishing boats surrounded the landing craft. There was a tense period now, for pirates frequently sailed in such vessels, and when the fishing boats made hostile moves, the refugees resorted to guile.

With no armaments on board, the refugees only had lengths of wood to thrust through their empty gun turrets and train on the menacing boats. Luckily the threat was enough; the fishing boats sheered off and sailed away.

Wallowing in the water, obviously in distress, the landing craft was ignored by ship after ship. After fourteen days at sea, with the children breaking out in cold-water sores, a baby was born on board. There was no privacy for the mother and there seemed little future for the child. But two days later, a ship stopped to help them.

This was *Bendearg,* under Captain Schofield and all the refugees were picked up and brought safely into Singapore. A feeding bottle was made for the new baby and the crew of *Bendearg* fed and cared for the adults, amused the children and, when they arrived at Singapore, raised a substantial sum of money to clothe their passengers.

This was a heartening incident in itself, but sobering to think that so many ships sailed past the refugees.

Occasionally though, a ship could herself be the survivor.

*Ada Liedale* was an iron built ship that carried general cargo. In October 1876 she was 2000 miles east of the Marquesas Islands when her cargo of coal overheated and fire broke out. The crew abandoned ship and watched their blazing vessel drift to the horizon.

It was June next year that *Ada Liedale* turned up again, still on fire. A French warship towed her into Papeete in Tahiti but it was another eleven months before the fire finally burned itself out. The French, masters of ingenuity, refitted the ship and sailed her throughout the Pacific.

*Ada Liedale* proved that ships could survive being abandoned by their men, as men could survive the loss of their ship.

# 13 Fighting Seamen

The Phoenicians were sea professionals. They were traders and slavers and mercenaries. It was Phoenicians who manned the Egyptian fleet which defeated the Sea Peoples in 1190 BC and Phoenicians who provided Xerxes, king of Persia, with his fleet.

An egoistic man, Xerxes ordered the sea whipped when it disobeyed him, and he built a bridge of boats across the Hellespont.

At first Persian numbers carried all before them as they invaded Greece. Thermopylae was a bloody victory over Leonidas and his Spartans; Athens burned bright beneath the harsh Attic sun and only the triremes of Themistocles sailed between slavery and survival.

Was that enough?

'The Greeks are better sailors than you' warned Artemisia, sea queen of Halicarnassus 'and their ships are better than yours' Xerxes should have listened; Artemisia had provided five of her own vessels for his fleet.

To Xerxes' 1000 heavily-laden ships, Themistocles had less than 400, but they were all Greek, lean vessels of cedar and cypress, brilliant in red and yellow, fighting for their lives. They fought at Salamis, with the temple of Athene nearby and the Greeks took the initiative.

It was a case of ram and board and when Xerxes' allies the Ionians broke and fled, Themistocles concentrated on the Phoenician contingent, the left wing of the fleet. That was a harder struggle and Artemisia battled harder than most. Her ships wore bronze armour and Xerxes said of her, 'Today the women are acting like men…'

Angered and ashamed at the cowardice of her allies, Artemisia changed sides and left the battle, a red torch flaring from her mast.

With both Ionian and Phoenicians defeated, all the Persians could do was die or run. They did both and the sea was filled with the wreckage of dying ships and drowning men.

This victory of Salamis saved Greece, and possibly quite a lot more, from Persian conquest. It was a warning of the coming of sea power and the beginning of the decline of the Persian Empire.

Yet the victor of this decisive battle, Themistocles, is not as well remembered as the adventurer Odysseus, or that other Greek of two thousand years later and a much more dubious lifestyle – Barbarossa.

There were actually two notable Barbarossas, the sons of a Greek coasting skipper and an Andelucian mother, and their reputations were as fiery as the colour of their hair.

Their first target was Algiers where they intended to rule, but that scheme ended when the Spanish killed the younger brother Horuk.

Tunis was next on the list and from here Barbarossa's corsairs plagued the Mediterranean. Although Barbarossa was also known as Redbeard, the Grand Turk at Constantinople named him Khair-ed-din, the Defender of Religion, but his method of defence was attack and his religion was a blend of debauchery and piracy.

When at last the Emperor Charles captured Tunis, Barbarossa escaped with his galleys and savaged the Christian reinforcements. He rowed to Algiers via the Balearics and took his many prizes to Constantinople. For upwards of sixty years he terrorised Christian shipping, save for a short period when he drank and womanised in France.

On retiral, Barbarossa resumed his given name of Azor and lived quietly by the Bosphorus, growing peonies until his death in 1546.

He had been one of the last old-style Mediterranean warriors and the battle of Lepanto in 1571, less than thirty years after his death, was the last major galley fight in history. Already seapower depended on sails and cannon, not oars and ramming, and men like Hawkins and Grenville would guide their keels through hostile seas.

Like so many of Elizabeth's finest, Sir Richard Grenville was a west country man, born in Devon in 1541. His father had died when *Mary Rose* capsized, but although at first he campaigned on land in Ireland and against the Turks, Grenville made his name at sea. It seems Elizabethan Englishmen could turn their hands to just about anything.

In 1585 he commanded a seven-ship fleet of colonists for Virginia, now North Carolina – a colony which was first abandoned then lost completely. Three years later Grenville led three of the English terriers which yapped at the sterns of Philips's Armada in one of the most intriguing naval battles in history.

It was a strange war that dragged out, with religion a cornerstone and riches a reason as English ships baited Spain with pinpricking raids. Plunderers became heroes and the English queen was more devious than the Dons her countrymen pretended to despise.

In 1591 Elizabeth sent out a squadron to seize a Spanish treasure fleet. There were four 500-ton ships including Grenville's *Revenge*, one of half that size, a barque, six armed merchantmen and eight small pinnaces.

Howard was in overall command and he cruised the Atlantic for a month before hearing that a large Spanish fleet was sailing to escort a convoy from the Americas. For all their apparent size the English were just small ships in a large ocean and after a fruitless search Howard put into Flores in the Azores for supplies, water and, possibly, wine.

With many of his sick ashore, Howard must have cursed the captain of the pinnace who warned him of the Spanish fleet. Fifty-three ships strong, the messenger said, and at Terciera, another of the Azore islands. Don Alonzo de Baza commanded this fleet and six of the ships were galleons of the latest design.

This was King Philip's reaction to the Armada defeat. Huge galleons, at 1500 tons more than three times the size of the English ships and, with sixty cannon, capable of blasting anything afloat. These were the dreadnoughts of their day, the superships, and Howard decided he had not the firepower to fight and withdrew.

Grenville, however, sailed the sixteen year old, five hundred-ton battleship *Revenge*, straight for the Spaniards.

Why? To protect the sick? Hardly – he had fifty on board. To give Howard time to escape? No – Howard's ships were capable of sailing rings round the Spanish. Perhaps Grenville just liked a fight.

He got one.

*San Felipe* was first to close, until Grenville swept her with bar-shot. Then *San Bernardo* came in with her massive crew. Grappling hooks sang and thudded and Spanish boarders threw themselves onto the deck of *Revenge* – and were repelled.

*San Andrea* was next; Grenville sank her by gunfire.

And then Grenville was not alone. The aptly named *George Noble* of 150 tons sailed to his side until Grenville sent her away signalling, 'save thyself my friend, and leave me to my fate!'

It was one ship against a fleet. Ship after Spanish ship ranged alongside and the batter of cannon killed the wind, until dusk saw *Revenge* a dismantled wreck with corpses manning her guns and blood draining from her scuppers. But still she fought, until shortly before midnight Grenville was wounded, and wounded again as he was taken below.

During the night, the red glare of muzzle flash punctured the smoke as *Asunction* joined *San Andrea* below the waves and two other Spanish ships were badly damaged. Only at dawn, after a battle that had lasted sixteen hours, did *Revenge* stop fighting.

Probably with more relief than triumph, the Spanish towed what remained of *Revenge* into harbour but, ironically, an earthquake later sunk both her and many of her erstwhile adversaries. *Revenge* had her revenge and Grenville remains one of the most redoubtable of all seamen.

Samuel Greig was a seaman of a different calibre. While Grenville led his own countrymen against their native foes, Greig had to train, lead and inspire the seamen of a foreign nation not at all renowned for its seamanship.

Greig was a Scotsman, son of an Inverkeithing shipowner and he learned his trade on merchant vessels before entering the Navy. In a century of fierce naval wars, Greig saw action under Hawke at the Battle of Quiberon Bay in 1759 and gained £80 prize money at the capture of Havana. When the Seven Years War ended, Greig was one of the original five naval officers transferred to the Russian Navy of Catherine the Great.

What Greig found was not impressive. Ships of poor quality and men who were badly trained and ill disciplined. The British set grimly about their task of modernisation.

In 1769 a Russian-Turkish war erupted and Catherine sent a good part of her navy to the Mediterranean. Two of the three squadrons were commanded by Scots; one by Admiral John Elphinston, the other by Captain of the First Rank Samuel Greig. From their base in the Baltic the Russians slipped south, through the Channel, across the Bay of Biscay, past Gibraltar and east to the Levant.

The Turks withdrew to their fortified harbour of Cesme on the mainland coast of Turkey proper, opposite the island of Chios, now Khios. Here, at the end of 1770, the Russians found them. With no reputation for seamanship, the Russians had not been expected to reach this far and all the world knew that the Russian Navy was in no condition to attack a fortified base.

All the world was wrong.

Supported by lieutenants Mackenzie and Dugdale, Greig led a flotilla of fireships straight into the anchorage. In the resulting melee all the Turkish ships were destroyed. Mackenzie was promoted to captain; Greig to Rear admiral and now the Russians could sail the Mediterranean without fear of Turkish interference.

When Greig located and destroyed a great quantity of Turkish munitions he smoothed his way up the career ladder and at the end of the war in 1772 he was raised to Vice Admiral. Now he assumed the task of dragging the Russian navy from its lethargy into an efficient fighting force.

This was harder than merely defeating the Turks but Greig put his mind to it. As governor of Kronsdadt he updated the port defences and created an entire new fleet. Simultaneously he began a program of training and restructuring the disciplinary practices of the Navy. Catherine was so impressed that in 1788, at a time when John Paul Jones was one of her officers, she offered Greig command of her Mediterranean fleet. Greig, however, preferred to remain in the Baltic.

That year, Russia was again involved with the Turks and also became embroiled with Sweden whereupon Greig found himself in the action. After a drawn-out battle, Greig died at sea, blockading the Swedish fleet in Sveaborg and he became remembered as the 'Father of the Russian Navy.'

In his career Greig fought the French and Spanish, the Turks and Swedes but among the most bitter of wars are those fought between people of the same country. None was more so than the conflict between the Unionist and Confederate States of America in the 1860s.

This was mainly a land-based war, but there were notable deeds at sea, with the duel between *Merrimac* and *Monitor* memorable as the first ironclad clash, and the exploits of the Clyde-built blockade runner *Neptune* not forgotten.

However, best remembered was Raphael Semmes. Maryland-born Semmes was known as 'Old Beeswax' because of his regularly-waxed moustache, and was perhaps the most effective raiding seaman in the war.

In 1861 the wooden-hulled, 900-ton *Eurica* was launched at Birkenhead. Barque rigged, she had a crew of 24 officers, 120 men and was destined to become a legend. Both the Royal Navy and the Unionists knew she was intended for the Confederacy but Semmes still took her, changed her name to *Alabama* and sailed into history.

With a 300-horsepower engine and eight guns, *Alabama* took the Unionist whaling ship *Ocmulgee* by surprise. There was a tense minute when the whalers reached for their flensing knives but sense prevailed and they surrendered. *Ocmulgee* was burned.

Eight more whalers were taken, and then Semmes sailed *Alabama* to the Grand Banks of Newfoundland. Here *Lamplighter* was captured, as was *Lafayette* and four other vessels. On the 30th November 1861 *Alabama* took the ship *Parker Cooke* and stripped her of cheese, butter, beef and pork.

More a commerce raider than a warrior, *Alabama* lived on what she could rob and when Semmes boasted that his men were the best fed afloat he was not far wrong.

As the Confederacy was always short of money, Semmes planned to capture one of the gold carrying clippers of the north. He chased and caught *Ariel* but she had only £10,000 and a host of elegant ladies. The money was useful but not enough; the company pleasant but incidental and *Alabama* continued her cruise.

For the seamen, leaving behind twirling parasols, coy glances and the curve of hip and cheek, it would be a sad parting.

Off Texas, *Alabama* fell in with USS *Hatteras*, a converted paddle steamer. Announcing she was HMS *Petrel, Alabama* sailed in close and opened fire; *Hatteras* was defeated in minutes, one of the only two warships Semmes had to fight.

Later when sailing across the Atlantic *Alabama* fired on a ship and was surprised when a shell arced back. Unused to resistance, Semmes asked who this ship might be.

'HMS *Diomede*' came the calm reply. 'And you are?'

'*Alabama*'

'Thought you might be' said the Royal Navy, and the two ships parted.

Folklore claims that Semmes had a base somewhere on the coast of southern Africa. History tells of his capture of a Union ship off Table Bay, with crowds cheering as he towed her into Saldanha Bay. The Capetonians made much of Semmes and a song was created in his honour.

*There comes the Alibaa-ma*
*The Alibaa-ma comes over the sea.*

Also close to shore was his last fight, with USS *Kearsage* off Cherbourg. After her 65,000-mile cruise and over sixty captures, *Alabama* was defeated. Semmes retired from the sea and became a professor, which was a strange preference for a fighting seaman.

But the sea is like that.

# 14 Fast Ships

In 1897 Victoria was the Queen-Empress of one fifth of the globe. From Canada to Cape Town, Caithness to Christchurch the Lion held tight the bonds of Empire. But for all its landmass, this was a maritime empire and the underpaid redcoats could not reach their scattered bases unless the Navy took them there.

So it was fitting that Victoria should review the ships of her Senior Service. Lined up in impressive array, the Navy waited off Spithead. It was large enough to dwarf any foreign fleet, and powerful enough to keep the seas free yet there was not a ship there fast enough to catch Sir Charles Parson's prototype vessel *Turbinia* as she surged between the immaculate lines.

Changes in nautical technology could be like that, outrageously swift and so consummate that all other vessels were outdated overnight. Parson's *Turbinia* created a demand for the steam turbine that had powered her, and revolutionised the speed capabilities of many ships.

This urge for speed was a fairly novel concept in maritime affairs. For centuries shipping had been content to slog along, often furling sail at dusk and resetting with the dawn, but the 19$^{th}$ century changed all that. Blockade runners, slavers, opium smugglers; all were built more for the speed on which they depended than for the safety which sea passages demanded.

Then came the clipper, a combination of many fine designs that arguably created the most beautiful vessel of all time.

Initially the United States of America built the best clippers with Donald Mackay of Boston producing a succession of tremendous ships. Vessels such as *Lightning, James Baines, Flying Cloud;* capable of 21 knots, built of light pine, broad in the beam for stability and with strong spars to carry acres of canvas, they rode the waves like ballet dancers, joyed at high seas which dismasted lesser craft and outpaced their rivals time and again.

Fine ships, impressively fast but too lightly built to last. Hard driving opened their seams, for softwood ships did not have the durability of the later British clippers.

By the 1860s, British yards were outbuilding the Americans and ships such as *Taeping, Flying Spur* and *Jerusalem* graced the seas.

These ships carried towering pyramids of sail and as much canvas as their masts could bear. Designed for a skysail above the main topgallant, many captains added a further layer of canvas. This was the moonsail, otherwise known as an Angel's Footstool or the sailor's delight although it was no delight to furl this on a stormy midnight in the Roaring Forties.

Even higher, on those ships where the mainmast stretched up to the scudding clouds, was the 'Curse of God.' Only the Lord was on intimate terms with the men sent this far aloft. Sealore claimed it took so long to clamber to the Curse of God that a clean-shaven sailor could grow a full beard before he returned to the deck.

Other seamen termed these topmost sails as moonrakers or stargazers.

Without a doubt one of the fastest sailing ships ever built was *Thermopylae.* Launched in Aberdeen in 1868 she was 212 feet long, a composite construction built of wood planking over an iron frame and all her 947 tons were designed for speed.

Like all ships of the Aberdeen White Star line, *Thermopylae* had a green hull bisected by a gold streak, elaborate scrollwork on bow and stern and white spars and blocks.

*There's a jaunty White Star Liner and her decks are scrubbed and clean*
*And her tall white spars are spotless and her hull is painted green.*
*Don't you smell the smoky stingo? Ech! You'll ken the Gaelic lingo*
*Of the porridge-eating person who was shipped in Aberdeen.*

So wrote Brady, the Australian sailor-poet.

From her maiden voyage *Thermopylae* was the ship to beat, the trend setter. When she took only 62 days from Gravesend to Melbourne the world took notice.

Then Captain John Willis decided to challenge *Thermopylae* with a ship of his own. In 1869 Willis's clipper was launched and her figurehead of a well proportioned woman in a skimpy shift was to become as famous as the poem which gave the ship her name.

*Cutty Sark* was eager for the race. As master, Willis chose a Fife man, Captain Moodie, noted for his ability to drive a ship hard in any weather.

'She was built for me and I never sailed in a finer ship' said Moodie of *Cutty Sark,* 'At ten or twelve knots she did not disturb the water at all.'

In 1872 a race was arranged between the two rival ships; Aberdeen versus the Clyde, the pride of Scotland to sail from the east of Asia to the west of Europe.

Both ships departed from Shanghai on the same day but *Cutty Sark* was held back by fog, giving *Thermopylae* a chance to be towed from the harbour. Immediately they hit open water the weather turned dirty, with gale force winds followed by fog, then an unforeseen and unwelcome calm.

Both clippers relished the monsoon when it blasted in on 23rd May, until a vicious squall tore *Cutty Sark's* fore topgallant sail to shreds. Even so, the clippers were level at Hong Kong, with 850 sea miles completed.

At the equator the ships were again within sight of each other, with *Cutty Sark* about eight miles ahead, a position she maintained until she encountered waterspouts and had to reduce sail.

Now *Thermopylae* closed, and off Anjer Point in Java she had inched ahead. Two thousand miles covered and not two hours of difference between the ships. A brief calm passed and on 26th June they were off the Cocos Islands with a stiff east-southeast wind. Always better in a strong breeze *Cutty Sark* forged ahead and in three days covered nearly one thousand miles.

During the second week of August the wind died but *Cutty Sark* upheld her lead, until heavy seas on the 15th tore off her rudder. To any ship this was serious, to a racing clipper in the middle of the Indian Ocean it could be a disaster. But the captain possessed an ace.

The ship's carpenter was Henry Henderson who had helped build the clipper and he manufactured a jury rudder out of old beams and a spare spar. Lowering himself over the stern, Henderson fitted this contraption and *Cutty Sark* was again mobile – but time had been lost. Folklore speaks of two stowaways, one a blacksmith, the other a carpenter, who made the rudder but it was Henderson who was presented with a certificate from John Willis himself, thanking him for working 'in a very clever and ingenious manner.'

Now *Cutty Sark* banged straight into head winds, almost unheard of in these waters. More delay. Not until September did the wind shift to the correct quarter, but fifteen days later, while in the Doldrums the rudder again came adrift. Again a makeshift rudder was used and *Cutty Sark* continued, now sadly astern.

On 18th October, after 115 days at sea, *Cutty Sark* arrived off the Downs to find *Thermopylae* had come in on the 12th; the Aberdeen ship had won.

Although the rivalry continued, the opening of the Suez Canal took the fire and purpose from the races. Now a steamship could perform the same journey in 50 days, faster than the fastest clipper, and the future belonged to steam.

*Cutty Sark* can still be seen in her final berth in London, but *Thermopylae* was transferred to the Portuguese Navy and used for torpedo practice.

*Caliph* was another ship built to rival *Thermopylae.* Her captain had commanded both and declared that *Caliph* was the fastest ship he ever sailed. Unfortunately she did not last long enough to prove his claim. On only her second voyage *Caliph* vanished in the China Seas. Perhaps a storm, an uncharted rock or pirates had ended her career.

The advent of steam killed those brave, dangerous days and the smutty vessels with their throbbing engines, their great turning paddles or screws, their continual demand for coal, oil or diesel, altered the face of shipping and the life of the seaman, for ever.

For better or worse? That is debatable. Easier? Possibly – but tell that to the stokers on an iron ship, half mad with heat in a tropical noon and their shovels still to ply. It was a hard life down there, without the freedom, or thraldom, of the wind.

When Parsons invented the steam turbine, nobody was interested until he embarrassed the Navy at the Royal review. After that people took note and orders came in for the new engine.

In 1907 *Mauritania* of the Cunard Line boasted four such steam turbines and she took the Atlantic speed record from its previous holder.

This record, the Blue Riband, was a prestigious thing and was so coveted that not only shipping company but also national prestige was at stake.

Germany, France, the United States, Britain and Italy were the main contenders. In the 1890s the Germans had *Kaiser Wilhelm der Grosse*, an elegant four-funnelled ship that crossed the ocean in five days, seventeen hours and eight minutes.

The *Kaiser Wilhelm* was a fine ship but *Mauritania*, which was built on the Tyne, was faster. Her record stood for twenty-two years until beaten by *Bremen* of Germany in 1929. Four years later the superb *Rex* crossed in four days, thirteen hours and won the honour for Italy. Then came the French; *Normandie* peeled the paint from her hull in her 1935 dash, but the European challenge was turning to other things. The excitement and sporting exhilaration of these beautiful ships with their ballrooms and crystal chandeliers, promenade decks and multi-course dinners ended with the turmoil of war.

Splendour at sea belonged to peacetime and the glory of the 1920s and 1930s was glossed onto insubstantial pretence. There was no peace in Europe, only an armed truce and after the savagery of the 1939–45 war, Europe was a sombre place, frightened of its own capability for destruction and ashamed of both its past and present.

Only America, brash, gaudy perhaps, but very much alive, faced the future with confidence, so it was fitting that an American ship should carry the post-war honours of the Blue Riband. The *United States* took the trophy on her maiden voyage at a speed exceeding 34 knots.

Donald Mackay might not have approved of her looks or her propulsion, but he would have appreciated her speed and stability. Even so, the fastest ship cannot hope to compete with the passenger jets, which have cut the journey time across the Atlantic to mere hours.

With these flying machines the need for speed at sea has virtually disappeared; only warships, rescue vessels and sporting boats need move fast, and racing merchant shipping belongs to another era.

Today the Blue Riband is a rich man's sporting trophy, raced for by little more than large powerboats and very few passenger ships cross the oceans on scheduled services.

But the glamour and delight of *Cutty Sark*, of *Lightning*, of *Thermopylae*, cannot be erased by time alone. In spirit, such lore of the sea remains in us all.

Eclipse *going through pack ice in North Greenland (1880s).* Reproduced by permission of Aberdeenshire Heritage.

# 15 The Explorers

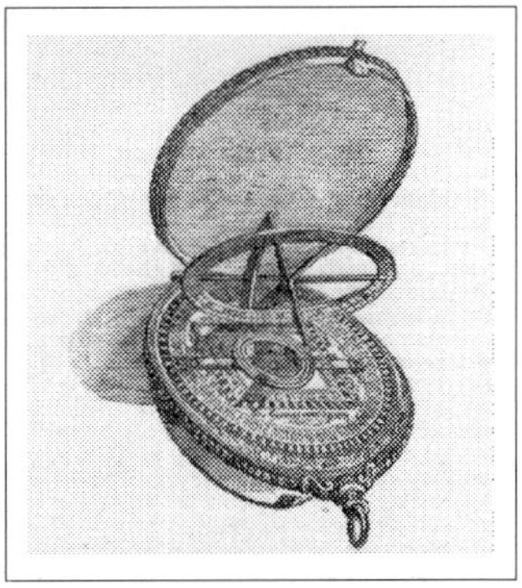

In the 14th century, when the mariners of the west scarcely dared sail outwith sight of land, an Arab traveller met the captain of a Chinese junk in an East African port. They spoke of sea navigation and the junk captain told the Arab of a far land he had once visited. 'A land of gold' he said 'so distant that the days of the voyage were uncountable.'

This golden land, the captain explained, lay far to the east of China but out there is nothing save the great Pacific and beyond that is America, North and South. If the Chinese had followed the equatorial counter current they might, after a voyage of uncountable days, have sighted the northern part of South America.

And that is not the only hint of Chinese exploration here. In 1975 a collection of unusual stones was discovered off the Californian coast. This was not a case for a geologist, but an archaeologist for these stones appeared to be of Asiatic origin and were possibly used as anchors. There was a possibility, no more, that the stones had once been anchors for junks from ancient China.

Did the Chinese discover America? In the year 502AD a monk by the name of Huishen told the Emperor Wu Ti of an extraordinary voyage he had made to the east of China – about 6500 miles east, which would easily have brought him to the American continent.

All this is maddeningly vague, tantalisingly possible and at this time, impossible to prove. We do know that Marco Polo found junks with fitted rudders and watertight bulkheads below decks. And by the 15th century there were multi-masted junks reaching 2000 tons in weight – Columbus crossed the Atlantic in a vessel of 100 tons.

With a fleet of such vessels, the 15th century Chinese Admiral Cheng Ho visited Burma, India, the Red Sea and East Africa. Cheng Ho stayed for a while and like any other tourist he shipped his souvenirs home, including a giraffe.

But if the Chinese were good seamen, they had neither the audacity nor the continual experience of the Arabs. Perhaps it was their knowledge of desert wastes that made the Arabs so much at home on the watery wastes of the ocean, but they showed far more daring and resolution than any contemporary European – with the possible exception of the Celts or the Norse.

There are four necessities for long distance sea travel. A sound ship, resolution, seamanship and navigation. The Arabs had all four and their reality was just as dashing as the Sinbad of their literature, just as colourful and had far more depth. The Arabs were among the greatest seamen of the world.

The Arabs were at sea before Rome had built its empire. They knew how to read the stars, and they combined this skill with a learned understanding of the monsoon winds. They had another advantage; rather than the oar-powered craft of the Greeks or the clumsy square sail of the north, the Arabs used the flexible lateen sail, which can catch and hold the wind from a variety of angles.

Arab craft regularly sailed to India and probed down the east coast of Africa. In time they pushed further, to the Malay peninsula and Sumatra. But mostly these were silent voyages, or at least silent to us. Few names have been recorded from these days although there is one that shines like a storm lantern on a moonless night.

Ibn Battutah was born in Tangiers and in his 30 years of travel he claimed to have visited all the countries of the Moslem world. Perhaps he did. It was he who met the Chinese seaman in Africa and he who described India and Mali, Spain and Bokhara. At the end of his memoirs, his secretary put in a footnote: 'It is plain to see that this shaykh is the traveller of the age.'

Which could well be true.

Yet in many things even the Arabs followed the routes of others.

In the Indian Ocean they cruised in the wake of the Greeks. The Greek navigator Hippalos pioneered the use of the monsoon and Greek ships penetrated to Barbaricum on the Indus, Muziris in Southern India and to Ceylon. Perhaps they also sailed to Oe Ed in Cambodia, where Indians met merchants from China.

In the Mediterranean, in the North Atlantic and possibly even off the African coast, the Arabs were preceded by the Phoenicians.

These unique, fascinating, terribly silent people were the professionals. They pioneered the seaways to the Atlantic. In fact, the seamen of Tyre and Byblos, Sidon and Sarepta explored virtually everything to the west of Sicily. Their high prowed, tar-black ships discovered the Balearic Islands, Sardinia, Corsica, Spain and then probed the exit from the central sea which had nursed, nurtured and contained so much of civilisation for so long.

When they saw the twin mountains of this exit, now known as the Strait Of Gibraltar, they named them the Pillars of Melkarth after the double pillars in the temple of Melkarth in Tyre. Melkarth was both a sea god and Lord of the Underworld; beyond the pillars lay the black unknown and only the Phoenicians dared sail there.

Unfortunately, in doing so they leave the factual world of exploration and enter the realm of folklore and fantasy. Under their guise of Carthaginians, the Phoenicians landed on the Azores. There was also a Phoenician settlement at Mogador on the Atlantic coast of Morocco.

But did Hanno really sail as far south as Senegal? Did Himilco batter through the Bay of Biscay to Britain and, most unbelievably, did some brave men actually sail right round Africa?

It was Net, Pharaoh of Egypt, who sent them on this voyage, and they followed the African coast for three years. In the autumn they landed, planted crops and waited until the harvest was gathered before sailing on. Unlike Hanno's voyage in which he reports elephants and savages and crocodiles, nothing of the circumnavigation adventure has been recorded. Save one fact: when they reached the southern end of Libya (Africa) and headed west, the sun rose on their right hand side.

And this, in the southern hemisphere, is true.

If the Phoenicians toiled up east Africa, they must have passed through the Mozambique Channel, which separates the mainland of Africa from the massive island of Mozambique. Around the fifth century AD there was a wave of immigrants coming here from the east. These people possibly came from Sumatra and settled in Mozambique. And therein lies a mystery.

Either they pushed off into the sun, hoping to find land, or they knew their destination in advance. To do the former would be a tremendous act of faith, while the latter meant that some unknown seaman had sailed the breadth of the Indian Ocean and then returned with news of his discoveries. So not only the Chinese were capable of sea navigation in the east.

Possibly even more intriguing and very much earlier was the discovery of Australia. To arrive here, man had to cross from somewhere in south east Asia, and this they did tens of thousands of years before Christ. What drove them to cross the seas? What boats did they use, and upon what experience did they draw?

From the area of south east Asia man seems to have spread eastward into the Pacific in not only one of the greatest maritime movements in history, but surely the longest lasting. To load one's family into a canoe, to pile on all one's worldly possessions and push off into the immensity of ocean took great courage. Brave, yes. Foolhardy, perhaps, and distinctly daring. These were people of the sea.

When population pressure forced them, the Melanesian people slipped into their Tainui, the double canoe connected by cross beams, hoisted their unique, claw-shaped sail, and headed for the horizon. Twin paddles steered them but it was seamanship that kept them alive.

From the Solomons to Fiji by 1300BC, to Samoa a few hundred years later and another thousand years to reach Hawaii. Then lastly to see the Long White Cloud of New Zealand and claim it for home.

There they lived, isolated and as secure as their own culture could conceive, until the northern Europeans exploded around them and their world was exposed for what it was – islands on a shrinking globe.

The peoples of north and western Europe were late to attempt transoceanic exploration, although there had been examples of their potential. To reach the many islands of Britain, waves of settlers had crossed stretches of water and in something large enough to carry their livestock.

Sea travel must have been mastered by the Neolithic people, for Orkney was an important centre from around 2500 BC, with Skara Brae being the best known relic of this period. The Bronze Age brought new technology and new people; bronze axes flashed among the dense woodland of the north and gold from Ireland was traded to the cool Orkney Islands.

It was a Roman fleet which determined that Britain was an island and 'Dispecta est Thule' – even Thule was sighted, but that was just about the only example of Roman sea exploration.

The Celtic Gaels made legendary voyages in search of isolation and the Lord. For a period, Iona in the Scottish Hebrides was the base for maritime explorations as intense and exciting as any in history.

Adamnan, biographer of Columba, has recorded voyages by curragh to the North Atlantic. Cormac Ua Liathaint took one of these blunt nosed leather craft 14 days into the unknown north 'Such a voyage appeared to be beyond the range of human exploration; and one from which there could be no return.' Cormac returned, but found no land.

Others did. Brendan of Clontarf seems to have reached the Faroe Islands, perhaps even Iceland and he is justly remembered as Brendan the Navigator. There was an Irish monk named Dicuil who wrote of extensive knowledge of the Faroes, Iceland and, interestingly, of permanent pack ice north east of Iceland.

It is possible that the Norsemen used the Gaelic experience to pursue their colonial adventures in the Atlantic. They may have followed the Celtic trail to Iceland, but it was a Norseman who found and named Greenland and a Norseman, Bjarne Herjolfson who became lost in fog off that island and ended 'Witless, methinks, in our forth faring' until he discovered a new land.

Eric the Red explored further and found a barren place he called Helle-land, a wooded place he named Markland and, finally, a land where vines grew that he named Vinland.

Whether this was America or not has neither been proved nor disproved but the folklore is both strong and persistent. The Welsh too have their claimant to American discovery in the person of Madoc, son of Owen Gwyneth, who left Wales after a family dispute and found land in the west. Legend says that around 1170 he returned for more men and then crossed the Atlantic a second and last time.

Finally there are the people who tied all the long legacy of discovery together, who created order from fable and a cohesive whole from a myriad of travellers' tales. If the North Europeans were late arrivals in the field of maritime exploration, they were also extremely thorough. No ocean, no sea, no coast escaped their scrutiny and if their meddling brought a great deal of harm, it also awakened the world to its own essential unity.

The catalyst for the sudden surge of European seamen was Prince Henry, called the Navigator, younger son of King John of Portugal. Born at the tail end of the 14th century, he founded a school for navigators at Sagres, where the rim of continental Europe kisses the Atlantic, and he encouraged his seamen to thrust down the African coast.

At fist there was reluctance; it was thought that south of Cape Bojados the ocean boiled; also that it was so shallow that no ship could float there, and fearful tides would ensure that no return was possible. Experience helped overcome these fears and Portuguese navigators inched south round the bulk of Africa. Eannes reached the Rio de Oro. Baldaya saw Cape Blank. Da Cadamosto sailed south of the Gambia.

It was slow progress but thorough and once a point was reached it was filed in the minds and charts of Portuguese navigators. Gomes reached the coast of Guinea; Cao got to Walvis Bay and then came the big two. Bartholomew Dias rounded the Cape of Good Hope and Vasco da Gama, one of the great names in exploration, sailed beyond Africa to the East.

With the seaways to the Orient open, there was no stopping the Portuguese and their caravels pioneered trade routes to the Moluccas, to China, to Japan and finally, they sailed right round the globe.

Although he failed in his personal circumnavigation, Ferdinand Magellan was the inspiration for the concept, but the man who completed the circuit was a Basque, Juan Sebastian de Elcano. In 1519 he left Portugal as master of *Conception,* and on Saturday 6th September 1522 he brought back the storm-battered *Victoria*. sole remaining ship of the five that had left to circumnavigate the globe. He brought home 17 men, the survivors of the 270 that had set out – and his name is barely remembered.

While the Portuguese opened up the east, their Iberian cousins from Spain reached west. Yet it was a tall Genoese redhead who made probably the most important single voyage in history. Christopher Columbus is an enigma; the great explorer who failed to find the land he sought; the visionary who understood the hardship of the sea; the gentle man who hardened his heart to mutiny; the man who discovered a golden continent and who died in poverty.

Whatever else he was, Columbus was a seaman and in his wake sailed the scavengers who scrabbled for glory amongst the riches he had revealed. Yet there were good seamen there too; Balboa who first saw the Pacific; Cordoba who explored the coast of Yucatan. Pinzon who traced the north west coast of South America and Amerigo Vespucci of Florence who may have had the entire continent named in his honour.

After the Iberians came the Dutch, superb seamen who rounded and named Cape Horn, who founded a colony at the tip of Africa, who braved the ice of the north in their quest for whales.

Then finally, the British.

The British were latecomers but nevertheless came to dominate the oceans and although Frobisher and Drake, Hudson, Ross and Chancellor may not have had the same impact as Da Gama or Columbus, Cook was surely the greatest navigator of them all.

But the European contribution was not limited to mere discovery. Virtually everywhere they sailed had been visited by somebody – an Arab or Polynesian or Carthaginian had already been there. European genius, European expertise lay in the charting and sharing of their findings.

True maritime exploration lies not only in discovery but also in revelation, in opening up the seas to the shipping of the world. At that the British were supreme. They charted every ocean, made those charts available to all and for a hard won century strove to maintain the seas as a highway of peace.

Since the fading of Pax Britannica, many of the coasts are not so accessible. Perhaps, soon, it will be time for a new generation of explorers to sail. And the spirit of Hanno, of Ibn Batutah, of Columbus and Cook and all the rest will be there to guide them.

*Painting of whalers crushed in ice – the 'Baffin Fair' of 1830 when 19 British whalers were lost in ice* . Reproduced by permission of Aberdeenshire Heritage.

# 16 Ghostly Ships and the Devil Sea

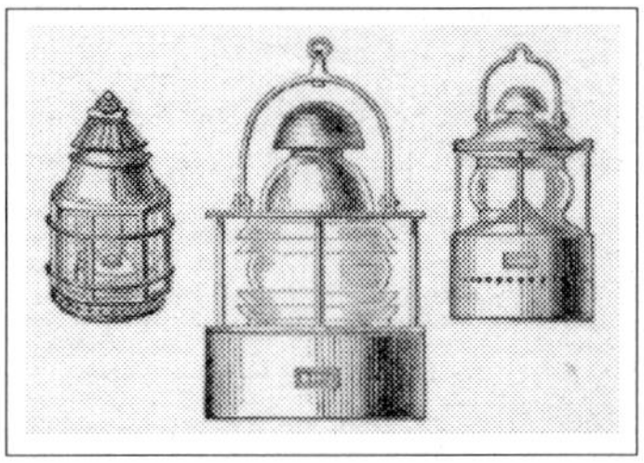

Sailing across a silent sea, the brigantine appeared a picture of peace. The square sail on her foremast flapped as the light breeze dropped, then she yawed, dipped her head and shook a little. To a casual observer she was a fine vessel, except for a few details; there was no ship's boat, sextant nor chronometer. But they were not needed, for nor was there a crew. This brigantine was adrift in the sea without a soul on board.

It was 1872 and *Mary Celeste* was found abandoned between Portugal and the Azores.

Much has been written of this incident, much has been speculated, from disease to sea monsters or little green men from Mars. It seems clear that the crew took to the lifeboat, but the reason why has never been discovered, and probably never will.

*Mary Celeste* was carvel built at Spencer's Island, Nova Scotia, and like other unlucky ships her name had been changed. Originally she was *Amazon* and her bad luck began on her maiden voyage in 1860 with the death of her master. Seven years later she went ashore at Cow Bay, Cape Breton and in 1868 she was renamed *Mary Celeste.*

Her new master was Benjamin Spooner Briggs of Wareham, Massachusetts, a seaman from a seafaring family, but also a family whose luck seemed to have ebbed with the tide. One of Brigg's brothers died in a shipwreck, as did his sister Maria, while another brother died at sea of yellow fever. His father, Nathan, survived his sea years, only to be killed by lightning.

When *Mary Celeste* left on what was to prove her final voyage she had ten in her crew, not the thirteen of legend, and they were steady, sober seamen, American or German. They had to be sober for their cargo was purely alcoholic.

It was Captain David Morehouse of *Dei Gratia* who sighted her first:

> *Brig* Mary Celeste *here derelict important send power attorney to claim her for Admiralty court.*

She had been making two and a half knots on a north west by north course with both jib and foresail set. The last log entry was dated 8am on the 25th November; she was found on the fourth December and although there was water in some cabins, and an unsheathed sword, nothing else looked untoward.

The mystery remains.

Other vessels have been found in a similar state but strangely, have not aroused the same interest. There was the *Rosalie*, for instance, which was found abandoned in 1840. Although all her crew was missing, the ship's canary was still aboard and unharmed. There was the *James. B. Chester*, fifteen years later. Again the ship was sound but her crew had vanished. In 1902 the *Freya* was found in a similar state.

Many of these vessels were found near that mysterious area known as the Bermuda Triangle. There has probably been nearly as much written about this area as about *Mary Celeste*, for the number of lost ships, boats and even aircraft must run into hundreds.

Columbus himself reported 'mysterious white water' in the region of the Bahamas, and spoke of a fireball which circled his ship before plunging into the sea. But any seaman venturing into totally unknown, uncharted waters with a grumbling crew and the possibility of no landfall for days or weeks or months, is entitled to be nervous. And tense nerves can play strange tricks at sea.

Interestingly, Columbus also saw a sea serpent in the seas off Hispaniola, so perhaps he attracted this type of phenomena.

To our modern minds, Bermuda is one of the more desirable places to visit with its fragrant climate, clean beaches and lack of pollution, but the men of *Sea Venture* thought otherwise. In 1609 this ship went down off the island group. Bermuda had not been in their itinerary, so when a longboat holding seven of these English colonists suddenly vanished without trace, the survivors decided that they did not like the place. They declared Bermuda was 'terrible to all that touched upon it.'

There may have been unsolved disappearances before 1800 but after that date they were better recorded. From USS *Pickering* to HMS *Atalanta* in 1880 the Triangle claimed eight known ships, but the 20th century saw this number increase tenfold.

Not only ships, but aircraft too, some of which relayed strange messages about holes in the sea. That has interested many people and brought forth pseudo-scientific theories about an undersea Atlantis and other bizarre notions.

Bizarre, unbelievable and utter nonsense. This is a tropical weather area where the North Atlantic Drift clashes with westerlies from the American continent and long tendrils of the Gulf Stream push through cooler water. All this creates sudden, unheralded storms, localised squalls and deep drops in the barometer. All this is nothing unnatural. This is an area made strange only by man's imagination. Everything else is a product of currents, storms, wind and the sea. Neither Atlanteans nor little green men are involved.

Off South Japan, between the Bonin Islands and the Marianas there is another area feared for the sudden and unexplained disappearance of ships. Like the Bermuda Triangle, this Devil Sea, or Ghost Sea, is known for its electrical storms and the malfunction of electrical instruments.

Perhaps – and this is only a tentative guess – there is some magnetic force in the area? A point where iron rocks beneath the sea affect a ship's compass and controls? Or maybe there are natural electrical disturbances responsible for electrical failure. No doubt time and genuine scientists will tell.

As a contrast to ships that disappear, there are some ships that refuse to die. By far the best known is the *Flying Dutchman*.

The basic legend tells us that in the 17th century there was a Dutch ship's captain named Van der Decken who bragged he could sail through any weather. He was given the chance to prove his words off the Cape of Good Hope when a south-easterly gale brought massive seas and a head wind.

The high superstructure of these old ships caught all the world's winds and the crew was terrified. They begged the captain to shorten sail. Laughing, Van der Decken began to taunt them, singing the obscene songs that seamen of the time favoured, and added a few blasphemies. This was tempting providence and the crew were on their knees, pleading for the ship to be turned back. Instead Van der Decken shouted for his pipe and a tankard of beer.

When the storm increased the captain raised his tankard and toasted the wind. When the sails were shredded, he laughed. When the masts snapped and the rigging whipped madly in the gale, Van der Decken jeered at the cowering hands. A deputation approached him and asked to head for shelter, but the captain lifted the spokesman and threw him over the side.

Possibly that was the final indignity for the black clouds were rent apart and a shimmering Shape shafted to the deck. Either God Himself or a being sent by Him, the Shape seemed to look at the captain who neither moved nor acknowledged the presence but with his cap on his head continued to smoke his pipe.

'Captain,' said the Shape 'you are a stubborn man.'

'And you are a villain' said the captain, lifting his wheelock pistol. 'Who wants a nice smooth passage? Not I! I want nothing from you, so go away or I'll blow your head off!'

The captain squeezed the trigger but his pistol would not fire and as he attempted to strike the Shape he found he could not lift his arm. But he could still shout and he called upon all his sea experience to curse the Shape. All the filthy, degrading things he had learned he used now, but the Shape was unmoved. Probably in his immeasurably longer existence he had heard it all before. Then the Shape began to speak:

'From this moment on you are cursed. You are sentenced to sail forever without rest or anchorage. You will taste neither beer nor tobacco. Your drink will be bitter water and your food red hot iron. Only a cabin boy will remain of your crew; horns will grow from his forehead and he will have a tiger's face and skin rougher than a dogfish.

You will always be on duty and will never be able to sleep. You shall torment seamen until the end of time. You will become the evil spirit of the sea. You will travel all oceans without stopping or resting. Your ship will bring bad luck to all that see it. And on the Day of Judgement the Devil will claim your soul.'

From that day until this Van der Decken has sailed his *Flying Dutchman* round the seas of the world, sending ships on the wrong course and terrifying seamen. As time passed he gathered a crew of all the worst sea tyrants, all cursed to sail at his side.

This tale would appear to be an amalgamation of several different stories, some taken from truth, most from tales woven in the long night watches. What would appear to be true is that a Dutch vessel disappeared somewhere between her home port and the Pacific. Less plausible is the fable that two Dutch merchantmen saw her wraith off the Cape of Good Hope and that she seemed to be weathering a heavy storm. Then there is the German story where Von Falkenberg, who was doomed to sail forever in a helmless ship in the North Sea, playing cards with the Devil, replaces Van der Decken. And that could be a corruption of another Dutch story when an East Indiaman commanded by Captain Fokke was racing to reach port. So intent was Fokke on being first that he diced with the Devil for speed. Now he is condemned to sail until doomsday in a ship crewed by skeletons, as he turns an hourglass to watch the sands of eternity slowly trickle past.

It was on 13th May 1866 that an Australian passenger ship, *General Grant*, sat becalmed until she saw an ancient full-rigged ship surge past. At that minute a mysterious breeze caught her and she was blown forward toward the cliffs of Auckland Island.

Thrown against the sheer rock, her jib boom was lost, then a current took her stern-first to another rock and the collision smashed both her rudder and her spanker boom. Spinning madly, the wheel cracked into the helmsman and broke two of his ribs but then the ship entered a massive cave. Her foremast smashed into the roof and fell, and then her topgallant mast and when the swell battered her mainmast through her hull, the crew finally abandoned ship.

Most of the crew died there and the captain was last seen waving from the mizzentop. Only ten people survived and it was eighteen months before they were rescued from Auckland Island.

Apparently *General Grant* carried gold and a later expedition found the cavern into which she had been driven. Three men entered but none came out. The remainder of that schooner's crew saw a full rigged ship ghost past.

There are many other vessels similar to the *Flying Dutchman* at large on the world's oceans.

The Goodwin Sands is a series of dangerous sandbanks about five miles off the coast of Kent. Legend tells of a time when this was fertile land, known by the Romans as Infera Insula, stretching to 4000 prime acres walled from the sea. William the Conqueror handed the land to the Abbey of St Augusine, Canterbury, but when the Abbot failed to maintain the sea wall the water poured in and by 1099 the entire area became the sandbank it is today.

On February 13$^{th}$ 1748, Captain Peel chose to honeymoon afloat on the ship *Lady Lovibond*. With the captain and his wife were selected wedding guests. Unfortunately the captain had not selected very well for there was a rejected suitor on board and he murdered the captain and piled the ship on the Goodwin Sands.

Fifty years later, to the day, a fishing boat was off the coast and saw *Lady Lovibond* again steering for the sands. There was laughter from the ship, the sound of a woman's voice and then nothing. Another fifty years passed before *Lady Lovibond* was seen again, then another fifty. She was not seen in 1948 so perhaps the ghosts are finally at rest.

Then there was *Palatine*, a Dutch ship that was wrecked off Rhode Island in 1752. After helping the survivors to safety, the Rhode Islanders looted the ship and set her on fire. Unfortunately there was a woman still on board and the looters watched in horror as she screamed for help among the flames. A ship, floating and on fire, has often been seen off this New England coast.

Typical ghost stories; meaningless, unprovable, entertaining. Or are they? Here is a log entry from HMS *Inconstant* from July 1881 while off the coast of Australia.

> *At 4 am the* Flying Dutchman *crossed our bows. She gave off a strange phosphorescent light like a phantom ship all aglow; in the middle of the glow her masts, spars and sails stood out in silhouette as she came up on the port bow where an officer of the watch also saw her as did a midshipman who was sent forward. But when he arrived at the bows there was no trace or sign whatever of any ship, near or on the horizon, the night being clear and the sea calm.*

Coincidence? Optical illusion? Yet the future King George VI was an officer on that ship, and he saw the *Dutchman*, as did 13 seamen. That the first of these men to see her also died that day might also be coincidence.

Possibly the ship did not exist but was a mirage, like an oasis in the desert.

Far from the Bermuda Triangle, the Arctic also has its tales of ships that disappear and if this is a different form of mystery it still baffled the experts of the time.

In the mid-19$^{th}$ century the hunt for the North West Passage was at its height. Since the days of Frobisher and Hudson, famous seamen had launched themselves to the north of Canada, depending on their energy and ingenuity to hack a passage through the ice and open a trade route to Asia.

It was May 1845 when Sir John Franklin led the latest expedition. He had two ships, *Erebus* and *Terror* and enough supplies to last three years. Intending to probe through Lancaster Sound and Barrow Sound, Franklin left for enduring mystery. His ships were last definitely identified in Melville Bay by the whaler *Prince of Wales* – and then they vanished.

Lady Franklin refused to give up hope for her husband; she provided both encouragement for official relief expeditions and finance for others. She encouraged some of the most expert polar explorers of the day to help in the search, but in the end she was disappointed.

Richardson took part, who had been on Franklin's previous expedition. Ross, who had taken a steamship into the Arctic. Dr Rae, who walked hundreds of miles and first found proof of Franklin's death. Pullen, who wrote of the ice: 'I can compare it to floating rocks which would go through a boat like a sheet of brown paper.'

Two messages were also found, declaring that *Erebus* and *Terror* had been abandoned on 22nd April 1848 'having been beset since 12th Sep. 1846' The same note had the sombre line 'Sir John Franklin died on 11th June 1847.'

Bodies were found; twelve at Starvation Cove, two inside a ship's boat and others, well preserved, at Beeches Island. Mysterious enough, but scientists may have discovered a reason for the deaths of the entire expedition. The lead content of the tinned food they were carrying may have been far too high. Lead poisoning may have effected many of the seamen.

And what of the ships themselves? Here lies a mystery which is easily the match of *Mary Celeste*. In April 1851 the brig *Renovation* saw some massive icebergs near Newfoundland. 'We met, or rather saw at a distance, one with two ships on it.' Reported her captain. 'One was lying on her beam-ends, with her deck toward us, having only her lower masts and bowsprit left standing. The other had her topmast on end, with lower and topsail yards across, but no sails bent; she had no topgallant masts up, and was nearly end-on to us...'

Possibly these ships were Franklin's *Erebus* and *Terror,* carried on the ice in which they had been abandoned. Two thousand miles on the current, it seems unbelievable, yet wreckage from Cape Horn has been found on South Georgia a thousand miles away and folklore tells of *Resolution*, abandoned in the Arctic and turning up off Cape Horn.

Tides and currents and vanishing ships all help to make the sea the interesting place it is.

The more modern Royal Navy also has its story of phantoms. The flight deck of *Ark Royal* was haunted by a ghostly pilot as, curiously, were the flight decks of *Triumph* and *Centaur.*

Here is one last ghost ship story, told to me by a seaman from Leith. Perhaps it will help put some of the others in perspective.

He was sailing round the Cape for Durban when a full rigged ship was sighted. White and silent, she seemed deserted and as the wind caught her sails, she slipped past the battered British steamer. Many of the steamer's crew were apprehensive and the name of *Flying Dutchman* was mentioned more than once.

Yet they made Durban in safety and there, berthed not far from them, was the ghost ship. A sail training ship from some foreign navy. Solid, normal but certainly white.

How many more have been like her?

# 17 Stormy Places

In the beginning there was the sea, and man wondered at the mysteries it contained. He experimented by floating things and by crossing the bays and river mouths to see what he could find. In time man learned how to go further and probed more distant coasts. And there he found fear.

Not fear of the deep water, for that could be navigated with skill, but fear of the places where the sea thundered against the land and ships were shattered on fangs of rock.

One such place was the Pentland Firth. The passage between Caithness and Orkney which connects the North Sea to the Atlantic is only seven miles wide yet tides here can surge at speeds of ten knots, creating such notorious eddies as the Merry Men o' Mey, the Bores o' Duncansby and the Swelkin. This stretch of water was known as Hell's Mouth to the old deepwatermen and they treated it with great respect.

It is said that some old time pilots boarded a ship at the island of Stroma and could not leave until they berthed in America. It was easier to cross the Atlantic than to set down a small boat in the Pentland Firth.

At other times the Orkney Ferry could be delayed for days, much to the frustration of the passengers and the delight of the local innkeeper.

This may all be true, but the weather in the Firth does not make it one of the world's most feared places to navigate. Three capes have this reputation, three stormy places whose names could chill the eyes of an experienced deepwaterman. These were Cape Guardafui in Somalia; the Cape of Good Hope at the southern tip of Africa, and the terrible Cape Horn.

Nowadays Guardafui is known by its Arab name, Ras Asir, and that may be fitting for the Arabs were one of the first people to weather this place. Ibn Batutah mentioned it, but it was the Portuguese who brought it to the attention of European mariners, who have cursed it, fluently and in many languages, ever since.

In 1909 the steamship *Temasserim* was wrecked in Ras Hafur Bay just north of Gurdafui. Thankful to be alive, the crew, including Miss Taylor the stewardess, scrambled onto the barren shore, only to see another danger as Somali tribesmen appeared.

This is a harsh place whose people adapted to the climate and the tribesmen intended to both loot the wreck and, more worrying, kidnap Miss Taylor. Possibly they had other things in mind as well, but the crew prepared to protect their stewardess. If they had been overpowered they intended to shoot Miss Taylor rather than allow her to be captured.

At the same time the second mate launched the surviving ship's lifeboat to sail for help. Weathering the Cape, the lifeboat ran the gauntlet of possibly piratical dhows and was picked up by a steamer as she approached Aden. From here a relief ship set out, and the castaways in Ras Hafur Bay must have been relieved to be rescued.

On this occasion the survivors were rescued.

Thousands of miles down the coast was Good Hope. To many this had been a dream, to others a nightmare ever since the ancient Phoenicians claimed to have circumnavigated Africa. But it was the Portuguese who put their keels to the sea and sailed south to their destiny.

Bartholomew Diaz commanded the expedition, which landed on the Orange River but a sudden storm slashed into his two caravels and he was forced south and west into unknown waters. After a fortnight of howling gales the weather abated and, as generations of Portuguese explorers had done before him, Diaz headed east to find land. There was none. Hardly daring to suspect the truth, he sailed north and came to Mossel Bay; Africa had been rounded.

Because of the storm which had masked the Cape, Diaz named the place Cape Tormentoso, the Cape of Storms, but King John of Portugal thought the Cape of Good Hope was more apt and named it accordingly. Yet to many seamen the name given by Diaz was correct for the sea in this area gives rise to countless storms. Here the meeting of the Indian Ocean with the Atlantic creates a confusion of currents and long swells. Add that to a southeasterly gale and tragedy is only one small mistake away.

Thirteen years after his discovery of El Tormentoso, one of the gales claimed the ship of Diaz, plus five other vessels of the fleet. Perhaps it is fitting that Da Gama, who sailed on to India, countered the Cape Doctor with an added prayer of his own, 'Holy Mother,' he pleaded 'take the helm yourself and do not let me stray from my course.'

The Cape Doctor was and is the southeast gale, which not only blows all the land-based germs out to sea but also raises monstrous waves.

Table Bay, where the Dutch East India Company settled, was wide open to the northwesterly gales. Not quite as destructive as the Doctor, but wicked enough. Sometime in the 1660s, the Dutch ship *De Jonge Thomas* was anchored when a northwester blasted in.

Exposed to the full force, *De Jonge Thomas* was thrust onto land and it seemed that the appalling breakers meant the crew were doomed until one Wilraad Wiltemade galloped his horse into the surf, time and again, hauling seventeen men clear. He did not come back the eighteenth time, but his name became a byword for bravery and a medal was named after him.

However, if he had lived, the Company would probably have prosecuted him for interfering unlawfully in Company affairs and salvaging Company property. Is it any wonder that the Boers trekked inland to escape from Company tyranny?

One day in September 1902 seventeen sailing ships and two steam tugs were wrecked by a south-easterly gale, all at Algoa Bay. Sixty-three men died that day, but nearly half a century earlier occurred possibly the Cape's most famous wreck.

Built in the 1840s, *Birkenhead* was a paddle-driven iron troopship. She had originally been intended as a frigate but had been converted and, to enlarge the accommodation, openings had been carved in her watertight bulkheads.

In 1852 South Africa was aflame as the Xhosa people fought against the British and *Birkenhead* sailed with red-coated reinforcements. On the 23rd February she called at Simonstown, filled her coal bunkers and loaded horses and stores. Two days later she headed for Port Elizabeth.

The evening was fine; light winds, excellent visibility, calm seas and *Birkenhead* steered, at eight and a half knots, onto a reef at Danger Point. The Cape had struck again, this time by stealth rather than storm. A combination of a deceptive swell and a strong current had taken the ship too far inshore.

A needle of rock had pierced *Birkenhead* and when Captain Salmond ordered full astern this rock ripped a massive rent in her hull. It is unlikely that the troops below deck were aware what was happening before the sea poured in, burst through the holes in the bulkhead and drowned them in their dozens.

As the crew struggled to free the lifeboats, *Birkenhead* broke her back, her funnel snapped and fell on the massed infantry on the deck. There should have been panic but there was not.

Major Seton, commanding the troops, ordered 60 men to the pumps, the horses blindfolded so they might swim to the tantalisingly visible shore, and the women and children first into the lifeboats. Not a single woman or child died. The men were not so fortunate.

With only three serviceable lifeboats remaining, Major Seton ordered the soldiers to form ranks on the poop. Many drowned at attention, others swam for the shore and if the thick seaweed hampered their progress, it also gave some protection from the circling sharks.

The schooner *Lioness* pulled fifty men off the mainmast but still over 400 drowned. 'Everyone did as he was directed' wrote Captain Wright, the most senior surviving officer 'and there was not a murmur or cry among them until the vessel made her final plunge.'

Birkenhead Drill became a byword for courage and a little more was added to the lore of the Cape.

But worse than Good Hope, worse than Guardafui, worse than just about anywhere in the world, Cape Horn thrusts its near 1400 feet of terrifying black rock from the southern tip of the Americas. The names here tell their own story: Adventure Cove; the Furies; Cape Desolation; False Cape; Dislocation Harbour; Cape Deceit.

There is nothing pleasant here, nothing to tempt the tourist. Only the great Cape Greybeards; mist, sleeting rain, ice and the savage green sea. Even on calm days there is a grim gloominess and the promise of coming nightmares.

Down here there is a roaring westerly gale for a full quarter of the winter. Channelled by the Andes, the wind blasts through Drake's Passage like a malign force that can pluck a man from the rigging or press a ship onto her beam ends.

Augmented by the powerful current, the sea can rise, then break on the shelving sea floor in breakers of appalling force. Waves of 40 feet are common, of 60 feet are known, and of 120 feet are spoken of. And by seamen, not fiction writers.

If an easterly gale fights the current, life at the Horn can be murderous. Yet until recently men fought the Horn in wind-powered ships. No wonder that, as a mark of respect, only those seamen who had successfully rounded this cape could cock their feet on the cabin able.

The early mariners did not face this. Most followed the route pioneered by Magellan; a narrow twisting passage between Tierra del Fuego and the mainland. Then in 1616 the Dutchmen le Maire and Schouten found the strait between Tierra del Fuego and Staten Island; the strait became Le Maire Strait and the southernmost point of the Americas was named Horn by Schouten, who originated in Hoorn, West Friesland.

To complicate matters, Drake had found clear seas even further south and although he never sailed it, the Drake Passage was named after him.

But finding the passage and rounding the Horn were not the same thing.

Not until Woodes Rogers voyage of 1709 did any British seaman write knowledgeably of the Horn, Woodes Rogers was an expert mariner and brought his ship safely through. His consort, *Duchess*, had a harder time.

> *...they had ship'd a great deal of water in lying by, and were forc'd to put before the Wind, and the Sea had broke in the Cabin-Windows, and over their Stern, filling their steerage and Waist, and had like to have spoil'd several Men; but God be thank'd all was otherwise indifferent well with 'em, only they were intolerably cold, and everything wet.*

Contrast that with the passage of Admiral Anson in 1741. For one hundred days his eight-ship squadron faced the horrors of the Horn. Only four reached the Juan Fernandez Islands, and these were filled with sick and weak men. Richard Walter, who sailed in Anson's flagship *Centurion,* recorded a poignant incident:

> *...one of our ablest seamen was canted overboard; we perceived that, notwithstanding the prodigious agitation of the waves, he swam very strong, and it was with the utmost concern that we found ourselves incapable of assisting him; indeed we were the more grievd at his unhappy fate as we lost sight of him struggling with the waves...*

Not surprisingly each ship's captain prepared for the Horn as best he could, checking all the ropes and sails, ensuring the boats and hatches were secure, or having sea anchors and oil bags ready to smooth the passage. Even so, far too many ships came to grief.

In 1893 the ship *Aethelbert* came close to an iceberg off the Horn. When pieces of ice loosed from the berg and crashed onto the ship the crew abandoned, only to see the iceberg floating clear. More than a little surprised, they returned on board and sailed free.

Others were not so lucky. One shipwrecked crew was found on Desolation Island, but too late to be rescued. Three pathetic clumps of white skeletons were huddled between the rocks. What story was not told there?

Then there was *Garthwray,* a full-rigged ship that left Grangemouth for Iquique in 1922. At the Horn she was dismasted by a savage gale. Returning to Montevideo to refit, *Garthwray* had to wait months for spars to come from Britain. Her second attempt at the Horn was no better; her fore and main topmasts were lost and she was forced as far back as Capetown.

Enough was enough; her captain, mate and even the ship's cat left. It was under a different captain that she tried again, this time via Australia. She reached Iquique but was wrecked on the island of Santa Marie.

Or there was *Carnedd Llewelyn* which was lost off the Horn in 1908. That was a season of gales and ice and *Falklandbank* was posted missing the same month. When the steamship *Devon* passed Tierra del Fuego she sighted fires but, supposing they were volcanic, she sailed on. Later two dead men were found in a ship's lifeboat.

Had shipwrecked seamen lighted the fires?

Strange things happened at the Horn. In 1922 *Hal* was abandoned off False Cape Horn when she grounded at the Hardy Peninsula. But as soon as the hands took to the lifeboats, *Hal* freed herself and drifted to the Washington Channel.

Days later, still afloat, she was sighted by an Argentinean cutter who sent a party to board her. But again *Hal* seemed on the verge of sinking so, at Hall Point, she was again abandoned.

Later still she was seen off the Hermite Islands and there, for the third time, she was reported as sinking. She was never reported again but had she merely evaded the sight of man to sail, unnavigated, around the Horn?

In 1891, Liverpool bound from San Francisco, *Dawpool* hit terrible seas off Cape Horn. When the main topgallant sheet carried away and tore the upper topsail, men were sent aloft to shorten sail. The sixty foot greybeards with their twenty foot crests of creamy surf were poised to poop the ship and Captain Fearon hove to. A thunderous cascade of water stove in the main hatch and when the mate attempted to secure it, a huge sea washed him and his men along the deck.

Gasping, terrified, the hands staggered to the foc'slehead and refused to move onto the leaping deck. Massive seas crashed onto the ship, pounding her, pouring through the gaping hole where her hatch cover should have been. Only the helmsman kept to his post.

The captain roared 'Come out and fight for your lives like men! And don't die like rats in a trap!'

With his courage broken and tears streaming down his face, the first mate refused to move but the second and third came out, and the professionals; sailmaker, carpenter, five brassbounders and two seamen.

This time they secured the hatch and saved the ship.

With the worst over, Captain Fearon brought *Dawpool* safely to port. It was this sort of night that persuaded many seamen not to sign on Cape Horn bound ships. These men, it was said, had 'Cape Horn Fever' and in time this term was used to describe any nautical malingerer.

So Cape Horn entered not only the folklore of the sea, but also the language.

# 18 The Superstitious Seaman

In the middle years of the 19th century there was a thriving trade between the ports of Wales and those of the Pacific coast of South America. These Welsh seamen were reckoned among the toughest afloat but even they were not immune to the superstition that the sea seems to create.

It was early spring 1860 when Captain Mathias took *Usk* loaded with Welsh coal, on the long voyage to Valparaiso. Somewhere in the region of Cape Horn, Captain Mathias had an extraordinary experience when the Lord appeared in person. 'Return home' advised the Lord 'or your ship will be burned to the water.'

Such warnings were hard to ignore and Captain Mathias ordered *Usk* back to Wales. Naturally the mate, as hard bitten as any, was both sceptical and unwilling, but he had little choice but to obey and in due course *Usk* berthed again at Newport. The curiosity at her return changed to amusement when the reason became known.

To prevent it overheating, the coal was unloaded and lay on the dockside for a few weeks while a new captain was hired. Then the coal was reloaded and *Usk* headed back to sea.

This time the Horn was rounded without incident but on the passage up the West Coast the coal began to overheat. This was always a possibility and the hands kept the deck awash with water to prevent a major fire. Unfortunately this only delayed the inevitable; by the time they reached Valparaiso the fire was in command and *Usk* was burned to the water.

Back home in his retirement, Captain Mathias would be entitled to feel some justification, although he would regret the loss of his old ship.

Were his actions due to superstition, or to a vision? Or was this the subconscious instinct of an experienced skipper emerging in a manner understandable to one living close both to nature and to God?

By the late 19th century many seamen were so religious that they refused to sail on a Sunday. There are recorded instances of ships lying idle, wasting the favourable wind that enabled others to surge past. In Scotland there were fishing villages which made no-Sunday-sailing a rigid rule, with all boats back by midnight on Saturday. On the other hand at least one East Lothian village claimed that the better the day, the better the catch and always sailed on the Sabbath.

In the west of Scotland even ferries were banned from Sunday sailing and there are tales of riots as day trippers attempted to land on those islands where strict Presbyterians held sway.

It was more traditional to avoid sailing on a Friday, the day of Freya, dealer in ill luck. There is a legend that in the late 18th century the government wished to disprove this hoodoo. The keel of a ship was laid on a Friday the 13th, she was named HMS *Friday* and sailed on a Friday. One version of the legend says she had a crew of thirteen, but all versions agree on one point: she was never seen again.

The story of *Austrasia* is more likely to be factual. It was on a Friday in May 1892 that Captain Parkes sailed her out of Calcutta for Liverpool and when he was reminded of the old belief in unlucky days he laughed.

Others were not so sure and watched the tall ship leaving the Hooghly with some misgivings which were, seemingly, justified. Almost at once Parkes found half a dozen stowaways on board and when a storm hit them that July there was extensive damage aloft. Both the mizzen and the foretopmasts were damaged and one man was blown off a yardarm.

After that things got worse; the main topmast was next to go and Captain Parkes, cursing, had to cross the Atlantic and put in at Rio de Janeiro to refit. Here he found the local dockyards unhelpful so the crew of *Austrasia* laboured to replace the spars themselves. It was October before they left Rio and December when they arrived in Liverpool.

'This comes of leaving on a Friday' claimed the owner, 'No more Friday sailings for my ships.'

Coincidence? Better not to chance too much at sea.

Sometimes it was not the day but the ship herself that was unlucky. The topsail schooner *Devil* was one such. Perhaps it was her name, or the fact that she was painted a sombre black, or the man sized figurehead of Old Nick she sported, but decent sailormen gave her a wide berth.

Her six-man crew did not seem to mind. They raised Hell in their home port of Preston, created mayhem at St John's Newfoundland, squabbled while on board and sailed her straight and speedy. So speedy that people muttered her namesake watched over her; six days from Newfoundland to Liverpool was some travelling for such a small vessel.

But if the devil provided her speed, he also sent his own weather for gales and driving rain lashed her black hull wherever she sailed. From the North Atlantic, *Devil* transferred her diabolical services to West Africa and here she disappeared.

Nobody knew how but rumour said that when her crew was kitten-weak with fever, *Devil* smacked herself into a sandbank. And there the devil met Davy Jones.

Perhaps that is what happened.

Of all the people who live by the sea it is the fishermen who most belong. Mainly they are born, live and die within sight and sound of the waves, their working lives are spent afloat hunting the contents of the sea and their pleasures are near the shore. In this profession, son follows father sometimes for generations so entire families, entire communities, became involved with the sea. And not just any sea; by necessity fishermen work in dangerous coastal waters, the area most feared by the deepwatermen who cross the oceans.

With all this legacy it is hardly surprising that fishermen have amassed a large stock of superstition.

There has long been a unique twist of logic in the Scottish psyche, a strangeness that combines the most hard-edged fundamental Christianity with a weird other-worldliness that does not disclaim fairies or second sight. So the fishermen thought nothing of lustily singing psalms while giving the minister a wide berth as they walked to the boat. Strangely, Catholic priests were not treated with the same horror; perhaps they were more tolerant, less inclined to interfere with the old ways. It was not unknown in the Forth Ports for cleansing salt to be burned after the visit of a minister.

Of course, ministers were not allowed on board a boat; even the mention of the name brought bad luck. 'Sky pilot' was used instead, or, more colloquially, 'the man with the black coat.' Just as unlucky was the use of the word kirk or church. 'Bell-hoose' was the substitute. In St Monans in Fife the very kirk bell was removed from its usual situation in the kirkyard when the herring season started. Apparently the clamour of the bell scared away the fish.

On the West Coast it was blood spilled by violence that frightened off the herring and perhaps this belief helped keep quarrels to a minimum. At an earlier age in the same area, blood was used to bless a boat, as a dead kid was hung from the mast. With that manner of blood sacrifice no wonder the minister was unwelcome!

Even more unlucky than the minister was a pig, or a rabbit, swan or salmon. A rabbit was known as 'furry-feet' in some places and it was not unknown for fishermen to deliberately not buy Swan matches. To counteract the mention of these animals, the fisherfolk had to run to the nearest metal object and say 'Touch cauld iron.' Curiously, iron was also considered effective against the malignancy of fairies, the People of Peace in Scottish folklore.

In the days when long lines were cast out of a boat, the starboard side was favoured, as that was the side chosen by the lord. But there was nothing biblical in the practice of sailing a boat sunwise while setting paper alight to burn off ill-luck!

Different superstitions related to different places, but always with the same theme: ill luck which affected the abundance or otherwise of the catch. So the walk from the fisherman's home to the boat was very important. For a Newhaven man to meet somebody with red hair was bad, as was the sighting of a black cat, or to have somebody else call out 'Good Morning' first.

The belief that cats were unlucky did not always apply in Shetland however, where the sight of a cat in front of a fisherman was good, unless it crossed his path. Then it meant bad fishing that day.

Fishing communities were matriarchal. The woman controlled her family and her budget with assurance and with the total confidence of her man. At sea however, it was a man's world with no woman permitted on the boat. This belief was extended in some of the Western Isles, with one fisherman employed in ensuring the shore was woman-free as the boats put to sea.

More widespread was the fear of a woman walking over a fishing line. Once again, that guaranteed a poor catch. Often men were also banned from crossing the line.

Sometimes the sea itself was used to bless the future of the fishing. This was around the Moray Firth where, on New Year's day, fishermen drew water from the sea and seaweed from the shore and took it home. To ensure good luck the water was splashed over the building and the seaweed placed over the door and in the hearth.

In the same area it was once believed that a man with webbed feet would never be drowned. Possibly this was some throwback to the Norse days, or a belief in mermen.

Another drowning superstition was not so pleasant but was certainly not confined to fishermen. If a man fell overboard it was quite common to let him struggle. The sea was owed a life from time to time and men had no right to take from her what was only her due. Many seamen did not bother to learn to swim – it was quicker that way.

Yet if a boat was cast ashore, taking a man with her, other fishermen from her home port would not set foot on the wreck. It was bad luck to board her, or to re-use her timbers.

Perhaps more superstitions were attached to the boats than to anything else. Although many seamen believed that leaving port on a Friday was unwise, that day of the week was the best for laying the keel of a new boat. And right from the start the builder would know if a boat were lucky or not – it could be sensed just by the feel of her.

Bread was considered the staff of life and whisky the water of life, and both were in abundance when a boat was launched. All those connected with the launch, and all those watching shared bread and whisky and a bottle of whisky was smashed over the boat before the skipper's wife spread barley flour over her.

In Fraserburgh all the apprentices joined their first boat in the water, being unceremoniously tossed into the harbour as soon as the keel left the slipway.

The minister certainly would not approve of the sunwise circuit a boat made on leaving harbour – this was an unknowing tribute to the old sea gods, long before either Protestant, Catholic or indeed Celtic Christianity was established in Scotland.

Even the ballast was important. A number of special white and red stones had to be included, and certainly no ballast from an old boat. Sometimes ballast could be very unlucky indeed, and not only on fishing vessels.

*Hinemoa* was a beautiful ship; one of the tall sailing ships built in such profusion at the tail end of the 19th century. Yet so bad was her reputation that men avoided sailing in her. When *Hinemoa* was built for the New Zealand meat trade, the latest refrigeration plants were placed on board her but unfortunately they proved mechanically unsound, rendering her cargo useless.

That was the least of *Hinemoa's* troubles. On her maiden voyage, four of her brassbounders died of typhoid and, although disease at sea was common, the presumed origin of this malady was disturbing.

Apparently *Hinemoa* had taken on her ballast from an ancient London burial ground and right from the start there had been problems. While running her easting down, *Hinemoa*'s ballast had shifted, smashed through the restraining boards and destabilised the ship. Now the crew blamed the typhoid deaths on germs from the same source; possibly plague victims had been buried in that London graveyard.

When some of the ballast was transferred to a local schooner, *Hinemoa*'s crew waited for disaster. When the ballast shifted, they just shook their heads.

Maybe it was just coincidence, but the masters of *Hinemoa* seemed an unlucky crowd with madness, drunkenness and death poised waiting. Two committed suicide, one was committed as insane, one drank himself into a mutiny and one ran his ship aground.

Other ships were just as unlucky. Such as the four-masted barque *Andorinha* which lost a man overboard on every voyage. Or the barque *Wanderer* whose beautiful lines were augmented by her figurehead of a shapely woman but whose life was marred by a spate of accidents.

One of her ex-masters, Captain Brander, retired from the sea but his old ship returned to haunt him. It was about two in the morning that the captain woke with a tremendous start. He had had a dream, he said, or possibly a vision, that his old *Wanderer* had been rammed by a steamer. In that dream he had watched the crew abandon ship as she slowly capsized.

No doubt there was some scepticism, even amusement, but that changed when news came that *Wanderer* had indeed been lost. While at anchor in a German port she had been rammed by another ship and had slowly sunk, turning on her beam ends as her crew scrambled to safety. And that had happened at about two in the morning.

Did the spirit of *Wanderer* remain with her captain even after they had parted, maintaining a firm and mysterious bond? Or was that just another coincidence?

What was the reasoning behind the old sealore of whistling up a wind when the ship's boys whistled in defiance during a period of calm? One legend claims it was a way of worshipping Cardea, the Triple Goddess who controlled the winds. To call the wind the seaman had to whistle three times while facing the direction from which he hoped the wind would come. As late as the 1960s, the Royal Naval Manual of Seamanship recommended that matelots refrain from whistling on board in case it annoyed their shipmates or interfered with the call of the bosun's pipes. Perhaps this voluntary self-control was related to the old goddess, or perhaps there was a relatively more modern explanation.

In the 19$^{th}$ century whistling on board a Royal Naval ship was a flogging offence. Not because of the ancient belief, but because of the mutinies of the *Nore* and *Spithead* where the mutineers passed messages with whistles. More obscure was the other superstition where a knife was thrust in the mast to bring wind.

The belief of rats leaving a sinking ship was based on fact, and a mariner would steer clear of a ship that lacked these creatures. If even the vermin thought it unsafe, what hope was there for humans! Incidentally, it was ship-borne rats which have been blamed for the great plagues of the Middle Ages, so rats were not pleasant at all, although in times of long voyages and scarce supplies they were often hunted for food. Conversely, if a seaman saw rats entering a ship he knew that the voyage should be trouble free.

French seamen liked to have a black cat on board ship as well, believing that this would charm away the bad spirits that drew a ship to her death.

Sometimes winds could be bought before a voyage. Northern lands produced wise women and wizards who had the knack of this. In Finland, wise women sold a length of rope with three knots. Untying one knot brought a breeze; two knots a strong wind and three knots a full gale.

The Gulf of Finland had a strange reputation for here the Finns could sail against the wind. While other ships were tacking and beating in the teeth of a gale, Finnish ships surged on with a bone in their teeth and all sails drawing nicely. Even as late as the 19$^{th}$ century Finns, known as Russian Finns, were believed to be able to control the wind.

In Orkney there was a famous witch named Bessie Miller who controlled the wind. For a mere sixpence she called up a favourable wind by boiling a kettle and saying certain charms. Very few seamen took the chance of neglecting Bessie Miller.

There were those who relied on their own superstitions. The privateers of Rhode Island never sailed until they had cast the horoscope of their ship. This gave them the best date to sail. In December 1745 they were told that Christmas Eve was a suitable day, so two ships left port. There was a powerful north east storm blowing that day and the Rhode Islanders sailed into the teeth of it, never doubting the accuracy of their horoscope.

Neither was seen again.

There is a uniqueness about sea life that makes the extraordinary appear normal, so what is considered superstition on land is only caution at sea. And while dealing with such a fickle element as the sea, caution is surely sensible.

And if that fails, touch cauld iron.

# 19 Blood Boats and Bucko Mates

To the old-time seamen the sea was their element, the ship their home and the captain their dictator. He had the final say in all the decisions that affected their lives: food, accommodation, work. While a good captain could make a happy crew, a tyrant would provide purgatory. Unfortunately there were many such men and each earned his sobriquet of 'bully.'

The dictionary describes a bully as 'a cruel and boastful oppressor of the weak' although, particularly in America, bully has a secondary meaning of 'excellent.' This is interesting for many, though by no means all, of these sea bullies were also excellent seamen.

It was the proud boast of many seamen that they had sailed with bully captains and as the Americans had a plethora of such captains, an American accent was adopted as proof – often by men who had never hauled a rope in an American ship.

Walter Runciman, the Northumbrian who rose from cabin boy to be owner of a fleet, writes of these times:

> *...the treatment aboard a tea-clipper was immeasurably better than that practised with pride by the officers aboard the average American sailing vessel, yet they (the hands) liked to boast of having sailed under the Stars and Stripes, where the belaying-pin, knuckle duster, and revolver were freely used.*

Runciman himself signed on in an American ship. He lasted one voyage before swapping Old Glory for the Red Duster. Not for nothing were American ships labelled 'blood boats.'

*We drank our rum in Portland*
*We've thrashed through the Bering Strait*
*And we've toed the mark on a Yankee bark*
*With a hard case Down East mate.*

A Down East mate, or master, would come from the eastern seaboard of America; a nasal-voiced Yankee, often with a tall hat and a penchant for chewing tobacco. Backed by tough, bucko mates, they pounded their vessel through the seas and pounded the crew through their work.

Their ships were shockingly, sparklingly clean, with decks scrubbed white by the constant effort of driven men, and ropes and halyards gleamed. But persistent sealore says that there was so much attention paid to oppression that good seamanship suffered. Better to learn more aboard a hard living, underfed British ship than scrub decks and be well fed on an American blood boat where men were battered senseless with belaying pins and the rule of law rested in the six chambers of the captain's revolver.

Runciman certainly learned more from the Geordie skippers of the North Sea. Uncouth, barefoot and illiterate maybe, but these coasting skippers knew every inch of their sea territory and understood ships and men in a fashion few bullies would ever comprehend.

Bully Waterman was possibly the most notorious of them all. In the 1840s he commanded the lively clipper *Sea Witch* and raced her from New York to San Francisco. When he created his 97-day record for this passage in 1850 he thrashed round Cape Horn in a bitter southern winter.

Sealore credited Waterman with padlocking his sheets and standing at the break of the poop with a revolver, ready to shoot any of the crew who wanted to take in sail.

With his reputation for speed assured, in 1851 Waterman was given a new command, the 2006-ton *Challenge*. When he left New York, Waterman had a full crew but most had come from Europe with gold fever and had signed on purely to reach California. There they intended jumping ship and running for the gold fields.

Ever since the strike of '49, California was the Golden State and half the vagabonds and footloose adventurers of the world seemed to be rushing there. It was not unknown for ships to lose all their crew to gold fever.

Well aware of this, Waterman knew there would be few real seamen on *Challenge;* perhaps that was why he acted so harshly on the voyage.

Before *Challenge* left New York, Waterman mustered his crew and railed at them. They knew he was a seaman, a Down East hardcase with a reputation for speed and efficiency, and he told them exactly what he expected from them. No slacking, no idling, no lubberly behaviour. But as the hands listened, the bosun was systematically scouring their dunnage.

He removed all the spirits, the revolvers and the knuckle-dusters and tossed them over the side. The points of all the knives were blunted. If there was trouble on *Challenge,* it would not be through drink and the officers would have the advantage of weapons.

Sealore claims that both Waterman and Douglas, his first mate, carried revolvers with a knuckle-duster heavy in their pockets. Perhaps the use of these, or the practice of 'starting' the crew with lengths of knotted rope, initiated the attack on Douglas off Rio de Janeiro.

There were four men involved and all had knives. Trapped with his back to the mast, Douglas could only yell and Waterman, on the poop, ran to help. Either he had forgotten his revolver or he did not need it, for he felled the mutineers with a belaying pin.

With a bully captain and an inexperienced crew, *Challenge* was bound to hit trouble off the Horn. Three men fell from aloft, two died when they hit the deck, the third fell into the sea and vanished. Perhaps one of these was the elderly seaman whose death finally broke the patience of the crew and when *Challenge* reached San Francisco they sought revenge for Waterman's hazing.

Rousing the local dockyard workers with tales of cruelty and murder, the crew pursued Waterman through the streets and only when the militia was called out did the rioters quieten down.

Waterman and Douglas were taken to court to face charges but both were acquitted. Sealore claims that bribery helped and the judge was bought, the jury coerced. Perhaps – but that appears to have been Waterman's last voyage. He became the Port Warden of San Francisco and lived to a surprisingly mellow old age, preaching Christianity to the benighted and possibly bemused seamen of the docks.

Captain John Sparks was another bully. He skippered the barque *Gatherer* with so much cruelty that she became the Bloody *Gatherer*. One seaman committed suicide by cutting his own throat, another jumped off the royal yard, and a third was shot by the mate, 'Black' Charley Watt.

Although the American vessels were renowned as blood-boats, there were British captains who were quite bully enough to be avoided. When Walter Runciman was a very young cabin boy, steering in a fluky wind his captain became agitated:

> *...the more sudden the blasts, the more violent were his tongue's efforts at me; but when he overheard me say that I could not help the wind shifting, he sprang at me like a wild cat, accused me of daring to answer him back, and simultaneously struck me between the eyes with his fist.*

Runciman was lucky as the crew backed him against their captain. However, to notorious captains like Bully Bailey, the displeasure of the crew would have been meaningless.

Bailey was the senior captain of the firm of Herron, Dunn and Company, and a perverse man who regularly beat up all his crew from the mate to the cabin boy. He made his name with *Dovenby Hall* and his violence and foul language were legendary. When his own steward on the homeward voyage from San Francisco murdered him, Bailey's wife and daughter defended the murderer. The captain, they stated, was so bad that they could not bear to live with him.

Captain Butler of the ship *Durham* was also ill to cross. On one voyage he chained up most of his crew and bolted his wife's maid in her room. On another occasion he tied up a Rio de Janeiro crimp to the spanker boom for two days. As crimps were notorious for shanghaiing seamen perhaps that was a case of the bitten biting back.

The Navy had a more organised approach to discipline, although brutality was not unknown. From the cat of nine tails to a stoppage of the rum ration, the ratings of the 18th and 19th century were under a constant shadow. Errant ship's boys could be bent over the breech of a gun to be caned in a procedure known as 'kissing the gunners daughter' and during the 17th century this was performed every Monday morning. Superstitious seamen believed that if the boys were not caned, there would be a foul wind.

In more enlightened times a miscreant midshipman might be sent aloft to search for the Swiss Fleet, usually just before dinner. Scandinavian ships had their own code, and a man producing a knife in a fight would have his right hand transfixed to the mainmast with his own knife. Left like this for a full day, it was unlikely the man would commit the same offence a second time.

Of all sea bullies probably the worst were the slavers or the blackbirders. The terror and disease and stench of a slaveship are well known but blackbirding is barely remembered now.

This was a practice of the mid and late Victorian period as merciless sea captains sought to bring a supply of cheap labour to the Queensland sugar plantations from the Pacific Islands. Perhaps it is fitting that the first vessel used in this trade was the ex-opium clipper *Black Dog* commanded by Captain Robert Towns. The cannibal islands of the New Hebrides, now Vanuatu, were first to be targeted, but the foulness soon spread until all Melanesia was at risk.

These blackbirders were at best unpleasant, at worst purely evil with navy deserters, failed gold diggers, released criminals and malcontented seamen manning the hunting schooners. Their methods were crude and simple; they sank native canoes and grabbed the swimming survivors from the water, or they raided villages for recruits, often beheading the useless.

The heads could be bartered for Kanakas – living native workers – as the superstitious chiefs used heads as a status symbol, much like the Iron Age Celts.

The blackbirders were resisted, by both the more truculent natives and missionaries. One Bishop Patterson was the best known of these so the blackbirders disguised one of their schooners as his to trick the natives. They snatched more Kanakas this way but as a reprisal, or by mistake, Patterson was murdered by the natives.

Bully Ben Pearse was one of these blackbirders, the first to raid the Fiji Islands and even among these renegades he stood out as a bad man. Sometime in the 1880s his crew finally rebelled at his cruelty.

Pearse's schooner was in the Marshall Islands when he was grabbed and thrown over the side. Swimming strongly and cursing with much malice, Pearse demanded to be hauled back on board but instead the hands threw his seachest overboard also. 'Sail home on that' they advised.

That was the last of Bully Ben Pearse.

The Royal Navy stamped out the worst excesses of blackbirding. The Kidnapping Act of 1872 gave the navy the power, and patrols penetrated the Pacific, finding many strange things, such as the schooner *Dancing Wave* which was overfilled with raw recruits. They were literally raw for there were 41 naked men and women packed onto her, from the man clinging to the anchor chains to the woman who perched, legs dangling, at the masthead.

It was a terrible time for the islands. The schooner *Donald MacLean* was savaged by a dozen Malekula war canoes off the Mankelyne Islands in the New Hebrides. The Granton-built *Stanley* was attacked at Dillon's Bay, also in the New Hebrides by fifty warriors armed with clubs and spears, shark-toothed swords and trader's rifles, and the crew desperate in the knowledge that five missionaries had already been eaten here.

That same vessel was later wrecked and 116 survivors existed on a coral reef. Many died and cruelty, courage and suffering marked the passing of terrible days as the Kanakas listened to the conversation of their own dead.

This is hardly the tourist image of the balmy Pacific which itself might be considered travel-trade lore, where beautiful maidens and handsome men sing on tranquil beaches. Explorers perhaps brought the harsh light of the outside world into this area, but cannibalism and tribal warfare were endemic before Cook, and the men of Melanesia were redoubtable warriors and excellent seamen.

And if the sea had bully captains, there were also crews whose attitude and behaviour merited little better. Chief of these were the packet rats.

*To Liverpool I'll make my way,*
*To Liverpool that Packet school*

The shanty 'Across the Western Ocean' says:

*There's London Pat with his tarpaulin hat,*
*And 'Frisco Jim the Packet Rat*
*Beware them packet ships I pray,*
*They'll steal your gear and clothes away.*

Runciman, again, had a word or two about these:

> *...there was another class (known as packet rats) which nothing but brute force could keep under control. They would defy both the devil and the Deity.*

A packet was a ship, usually a sailing ship, which plied a regular route between two ports. The most notorious for bellicose crews was between Liverpool and New York. One of the best known and best avoided lines here was the Black Ball line. Here bully captains and bucko mates used 'belaying-pin soup' and constant cruelty to control the rats under their command.

Using the same tactics as Bully Waterman, the captain would call the men aft for a lecture while the mate ransacked the foc'sle. All liquor bottles were confiscated or smashed, all weapons were removed and the points of seaknives broken or blunted.

The packet rats frequently came on board with little more than the clothes they wore. They would quarrel over nothing; fight for fun and if they received little mercy from the captain, even that was more than they ever bestowed. Hard and tough, they sailed the packet ships into the worst that the Atlantic had to offer and came back for more.

Possibly even more violent than the packet rats was the crew picked up at San Francisco by *Leicester Castle* in 1902. Most of them had been obtained by crimps; shanghaied men with no desire to go to sea and less inclination to work.

Deep in the Pacific, hundreds of miles from even the nearest island, three of these reluctant seamen mutinied. It had been planned in advance, with a raft made ready for escape and pistols handy for defence. The mate was shot dead and Captain Peattie, a Paisley man, attempted to intervene. He was shot too, five times, and then the mutineers jumped onto their raft.

Perhaps they reached some island, possibly they did not but within a day Captain Peattie was back in command and he brought *Leicester Castle* safely to port. In Queenstown, Tasmania, four bullets were dug out of his body.

He was no bully captain but as an example of a tough seaman, Peattie would be hard to equal.

# 20 Drink and the Seaman

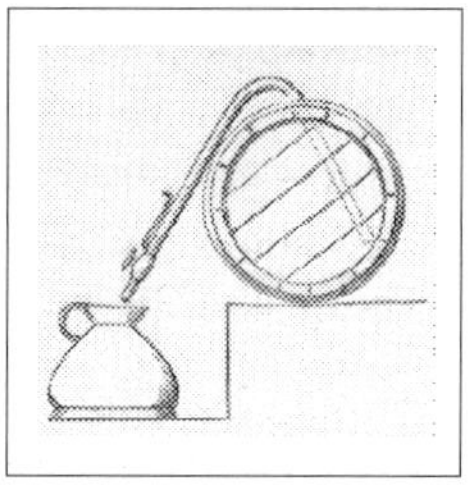

There is a rapport between seamen and drink which stretches back centuries exemplified by Ancaeus, helmsman of Jason's ship *Argo*, who liked his wine. When a slave prophesised that Ancaeus would not live to enjoy the product of his own vineyard, the helmsman only laughed and lifted a cupful. 'There's many a slip twixt the cup and the lip' warned the slave, and before Ancaeus could drink he was called away to hunt the Calydonian boar, which killed him.

Wine or other alcoholic drink, was an essential element in the stores of any ship and when James IV great *Michael* was laden she carried a staggering 7250 gallons of wine. Incidentally, she also carried salted porpoise, which is intriguing.

Andrew Wood, one of the outstanding captains of this period, had his crew toast each other with wine before his epic battle in the Forth in 1490, and his English opponent did the same.

In English ships of the 16$^{th}$ and 17$^{th}$ centuries, every seaman was issued four tots of beer each day. As each tot equalled two pints, that meant a full gallon of beer a day. This was excellent in home waters but less pleasant on a long voyage when the beer would invariably turn sour. If beer was scarce the captain could add water to make a drink known as 'swipes'.

As time passed and the West Indian sugar islands were acquired for the Empire, the rapture of rum was introduced and became a firm favourite. It warmed in a cool climate, kept better than beer, was more potent than wine and was fairly cheap to make.

Seamen much preferred rum to wine, although both were used. Wine was normally rationed to one pint per man per day. In the Caribbean it was either a pint of wine or half a pint of rum, while off North America the local spruce beer was issued.

There were many phrases invented to describe seamen's drink. They termed pure rum as 'pure north' and undiluted water as 'due west' so a mixture of half rum, half water was 'north west' while 'north west by west' would be one part water, two parts rum.

It was Admiral Vernon, veteran of Gibraltar, Malaga and Portobello, who advocated watering down the neat rum that had been served to the men. As the Admiral was nicknamed 'Old Grog' from the grogram coat he habitually wore, this watered rum became known as grog.

Rather than a gallon of beer, it became traditional for the Navy to issue one quart of grog a day, mixed with three pints of water. To the tune 'Nancy Dawson' this was served in two equal doses, at 12 noon and 4:30pm. Later these highlights of the seaman's life were cut by half as grog was only issued at noon. It was not until August 1970 that the Navy stopped issuing grog and the nickname of the Admiral responsible, Sir Michael Le Fanu, was probably less repeatable.

'Up Spirits' was one of the most powerful inducements to recruitment among men with a constant thirst. Grog became an accepted form of currency aboard the king's ships and although this was frowned upon by authority, many debts were paid by this means. A man on his birthday was awarded 'sippers', a taste from the grog of everybody on his mess. A favour, however, could be rewarded by 'gulpers', a mouthful while 'half a tot' was for something special. Only in exceptional cases such as life saving would the entire tot be surrendered!

Often, on a long cruise, rum or other drink was used to revitalise the stored water which could either be stale or a green home to many tiny living things.

'O! for a draught of fresh water I cry out' wrote young Bernard Coleridge to his mother in June 1804 'for our water stinkes enough to poison a person and we are generally forced to drink two glasses of wine or brandy to one glass of water to take off the stink.'

Woodes Rogers, who rescued Alexander Selkirk from Juan Fernandez, had no illusions about the importance of alcohol to the hands.

> *...at the same time we had but a slender stock of liquor, and our Men but meanly clad, yet good Liquour to Sailors is more preferable to Clothes.*

In Scotland, when a ship slid down the slipway, apprentices were given a 'launchbowl' and then intimidated the locality, pressing drink on any person they met.

Until the end of the 18th century, warships were christened with a bottle of port and the person performing the launch blessed himself with a preparatory glass. With such a start in life it is hardly surprising that drink played such a large part in naval folklore.

There was the case of HMS *Glasgow* for instance, whose rum caught fire as it was stored in the hold. Or the occasion when HMS *Culloden* ran aground and would not refloat until some of her heavy equipment was removed. Captain Edward Pellew hailed the first ship that passed, hoping to load *Culloden*'s cannon on board, but soon wished he had not bothered. The ship had a cargo of arrack, brandy and rum and in spite of all the officers' endeavours, most of *Culloden*'s crew were soon drunk and incapable.

Admiral Keith was only too aware of this weakness of the British seaman. 'Almost every crime except theft' he wrote to the Admiralty in 1812 'originates in drunkenness.' And he continued, 'a large proportion of the men who are maimed and disabled are reduced to their situation by accidents that happen from the same abominable vice.'

At least one lower deck hand would have agreed with that. John Bechervaise served at a later period and he wrote:

> *The man who writes these lines would not drink one glass of ardent spirits though the empty glass were to be given him full of sovereigns. The many punishments I saw inflicted on my first joining the service, for crimes committed in drunkenness, induced me to say that I never while I breathe would taste spirits.*

Even in a service as tightly disciplined as the Royal Navy, drunken seamen could be dangerous. After the battle of Trafalgar, prize crews of a couple of score of men under a junior lieutenant were sent aboard the captured enemy vessels. Often there was a dash for the drink in the prize ship and the officer could find himself with an intoxicated, useless prize crew, a damaged ship and a resentful horde of prisoners.

When the Navy boarded *Monarea*, two officers had to control 500 prisoners with 55 drunken British seamen. It is hardly surprising that one midshipman claimed he had been more afraid in the prize than in the battle.

One of the most enduring and intriguing pieces of sealore is also from the aftermath of Trafalgar. Mariners who died on board ship were commonly buried at sea, slid into the water with a cannonball at their feet and a short prayer said over them.

Admiral Nelson was treated with more reverence. He was returned to Britain for a state funeral. A Doctor Beatty was given the task of keeping Nelson's body in good condition until the funeral, so he placed the admiral in a leaguer – a large cask – filled with brandy. This was placed on its end in the middle deck of *Victory,* with a marine sentry constantly on guard.

Either the sentry was lax, or folklore has transformed possibility into reality, for a persistent story claims that the hands tapped the cask and drank the brandy. A misconception that the preservative was not brandy but rum has led to the latter being termed 'Nelsons blood' which has become a term of great respect.

This incident also led to the saying 'to tap the admiral' meaning to secretly broach a keg of spirits. Possibly there is some truth in the legend, for Nelson was afterwards placed in a lead coffin, also filled with brandy, with the addition of camphor and myrtle.

The close association between seamen and drink has given birth to many such expressions such as 'bulling the teapot.' Although this could mean making a second brew of tea, it comes from the old practice of swilling out a nearly-empty keg with water; the resulting mixture was referred to as 'bull' and was a very inferior drink.

Then there is 'three sheets in the wind' meaning drunk. A sheet is the rope fastened to the clew, or corner of a sail, which was used for trimming that sail. If the sheet is not secured, the sail will flap; it will be 'in the wind.' A seaman with one sheet in the wind was merry, not quite sober. Three sheets in the wind meant drunk and incapable.

To 'splice the mainbrace' meant to issue an extra tot of grog to the crew. This was very unusual and, as the mainbrace was the brace connected to the main yard, to splice this would be just as rare.

'Sucking the Monkey' is another purely nautical phrase. There are two similar meanings. Either spirits could be sucked from a cask by means of a straw, or rum drunk from the hollow shell of a coconut.

To the hard-living seamen who manned the tall ships of the 19$^{th}$ century, drink was one of the few redeeming features in life. Perhaps that was why British seamen had a terrible reputation for drunken violence and some ports on the Pacific seaboard of South America had specially-constructed steel cages purely for the containment of British seamen.

Sometimes the men did not even reach that far.

Around the turn of the 20$^{th}$ century the full-rigged *Lyderhorn* left Liverpool for Vancouver. At some time in the voyage the crew realised that there was liquor in the cargo and then it was only a matter of time before they sampled the stuff.

After a few days of controlling a drunken crew the captain clapped some in irons, dumped the remainder at a friendly port and took on a dozen South Americans to make up the balance. This was fine until *Lyderhorn* reached the foul weather off Cape Horn and the replacements mutinied.

As the officers quelled the ensuing riot, one of the hands was seriously wounded and seven others injured. When they reached Pernambuco, well short of Vancouver, most of the crew was in irons.

Seamen ashore in Britain were just as wild as when overseas. Folklore tells of early naval seamen who spent their prize money to buy watches, and then fried them in public to display their wealth. There are tales of seamen spending a year's wages in a binge that lasted for a week, and of seamen lying drunk in the gutter. Yet there are also accounts of incredible generosity with seamen giving handfuls of gold coins to beggars. And tales of men spending a night with street women who first relieved them of all their money and then sold them to a crimp.

*Now all you bully sailormen take warning when ashore*
*Or else you'll meet some charming gal who's nothing but a whore*
*Your hard earned cash will disappear, your rig and boots as well*
*For Yankee gals are tougher than the other side of Hell!*

Often the seaman was left with worse things than a sore head. In the dock areas of London, doss houses for seamen were sordidly simple; a single cellar with a rope stretching from wall to wall. The seaman, sober or probably drunk, suspended his upper half across the rope and slept like that.

There were also the pubs. In East London the Ratcliffe Road was a seaman's haunt where 'The Black Sheep' and 'Shakespeare' were known for cheap drink and friendly women. Near Faversham in Kent is the Shipwright's Arms', which was so well liked by the old time seamen that one remained to haunt the place. His reefer jacket and glaring eyes are still seen, occasionally.

Bristol has a couple of fascinating taverns in the 'Hole in the Wall' which is said to be the original of the Spyglass Inn in *Treasure Island*, and the Clandoger Trow Inn where Daniel Defoe met Alexander Selkirk.

Leith has the Old Chain Pier. Built in the 1960s for ferry traffic in the Firth of Forth, this pub was still raucous with Ma Moss reigning supreme. Imagine a landlady with bamboo framed spectacles who ushered troublemakers and late drinkers from her bar with a cutlass and was known to fire a pistol to prove her point? Half the mariners of Leith called in here, and sent presents and souvenirs from distant ports to prove their affection for old Ma Moss.

Probably drink did a lot of harm to seamen, but it added quite a spalsh of colour too!

# Glossary

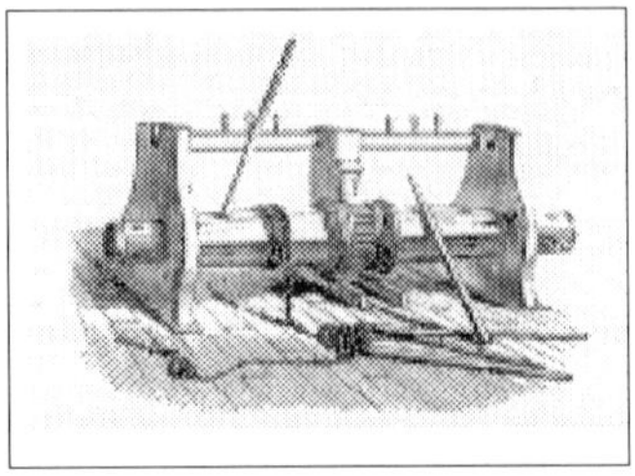

| | |
|---|---|
| **Arrack** | Intoxicating spirit, mainly from the east. |
| **Barque** | Three masted vessel whose mizzenmast is fore and aft rigged. |
| **Batten** | An iron bar used to secure the tarpaulin cover over a hatch. Usually several were used. |
| **Batten down** | Make secure. |
| **Beam** | The width of the hull. If a ship is on her beam-ends she is lying on her side. |
| **Belaying pin** | A length of wood or iron to which ropes could be fastened. |
| **Bitts** | Posts on a ship's deck used for fastening cables. |
| **Blubber boat/ship** | Whaling ship. |
| **Blockade runner** | Fast vessel used to carry supplies to a port under an enemy blockade. |
| **Boom** | The spar to which the foot of a sail is secured. |
| **Brassbounder** | Apprentice officer in 19th century merchant navy. The name comes from the gold lace binding round his cap. |
| **Brig** | A two-masted, square-rigged vessel. |
| **Brigantine** | A two-masted vessel with fore and aft sails on the mainmast. |
| **Bulkhead** | A partition; a wall inside a ship. |
| **Bulwark** | The side of a ship above the deck. |
| **Bum boat** | Boat that carried waste from a ship and brought back provisions of various sorts. Possibly from the Dutch boomboat, a broad-beamed fishing boat. |
| **Capstan bar** | Bars used on the machine that wound up a ship's cable. |
| **Caravel** | Type of 15th century ship used for ocean voyages. |
| **Carvel** | Method of ship construction where planks were laid end on end for a smooth finish. |
| **Caulk** | Oakum or something similar pressed into seams between planks to render ship waterproof. |
| **Cay** | Small island, common in Caribbean. |
| **Clinker** | Method of ship construction where one plank overlaps the next. |
| **Coble** | A small fishing boat. |
| **Corsair** | Pirate, privateer, especially of North Africa. |
| **CQD** | Come Quickly Danger. |

| | |
|---|---|
| **Flag ship** | The ship of a commodore or admiral, which carries his flag. |
| **Fo'csle** | The forecastle. In the Middle Ages the raised 'castle' at the bow of a ship. More commonly, the forepart of a ship where the crew live. |
| **Foremast** | The forward mast of a ship. |
| **Foremast hand** | Ordinary seaman. |
| **Galleon** | Fast, lean sailing ship of 16th century. |
| **Galley** | Oar powered warship, usually long and low. |
| **Greybeard** | Huge waves off Cape Horn, often fringed with foam. |
| **Halyard** | the rope by which a sail or yard is hauled up the mast. |
| **Headwind** | Wind from dead ahead; very difficult to sail into. |
| **Helm** | Wheel or tiller that controls the rudder and thus steers the ship. |
| **Holystone** | Rough oblong of pumice or similar, used to scrub decks. It was known as the Holystone or Seaman's Bible because the man was on his knees when using it. A smaller version for places where access was more difficult was known as a Prayerbook. |
| **Jury** (rig) | Temporary replacement to enable a ship to reach port where more permanent repairs could be made. |
| **Keel** | The backbone of a ship; the part which extends along the bottom of ship from bow to stern. |
| **Ketch** | A two-masted vessel; tall mainmast, short mizzen. |
| **King's Shilling** | Shilling coin given as a token of the recipient now being in H.M. Forces. |
| **Lateen** | Rig with a slanted yard and large triangular sail on short mast. From the French latine (Latin) due to its commonness in the Mediterranean. |
| **Levant** | Eastern coast of the Mediterranean. |
| **Lodestone** | Magnetic iron ore used as early compass. |
| **Longboat** | Largest of a ship's boats. Open rowing craft of Viking period. |
| **Lubber** | Unseamanlike. Awkward. Slovenly. |
| **Lymphad** | Hebridean galley of more than 16 oars. |
| **Mainmast** | The principal mast on ship, second from the bow if the heights are even. |
| **Mainsail** | The largest sail. Above this were the topsail, topgallant and royal skysail. |
| **Mainyard** | Yard to which mainsail is secured. |
| **Midshipman** | Lowest rank of commissioned officer. Now used only in shore-based training. |
| **Midships** | Middle of the ship. |
| **Mizzenmast** | Third mast in a ship. Fore, main, mizzen, spanker. |
| **Monsoon** | Indian Ocean wind system blowing SW from April to October; NE at other times. |
| **Orlop** | Lowest deck on a ship. |
| **Petty Officer** | Naval Non-Commissioned Officer |
| **Pinnace** | Small vessel powered by both sails and oars. |
| **Privateer** | Private vessel licensed to attack ships of opposing nation. |

| | |
|---|---|
| **Prize** | One ship captured by another. |
| **Prizemoney** | The proceeds from the sale of a prize ship and cargo. |
| **Prow** | The forepart of a vessel. |
| **Reef** | To reduce area of sail exposed to wind. |
| **Sea anchor** | Object placed in water and attached to vessel in order to increase drag and slow or halt progress. |
| **Sea People** | Translation of Egyptian name for the hordes of people who invaded the Levant in the 1180s BC; the Philistines of the Bible. |
| **Schooner** | Fore and aft-rigged vessel with two or more masts. |
| **Screw** | The propeller of a ship. |
| **Sheet** | Line secured to the lower corner of a square sail, or the aft corner of a fore and aft sail. |
| **Siren** | Mythical creature who used beautiful music to entice seamen into danger. |
| **Slow match** | Slow-burning fuse used for firing cannon, etc. |
| **Spar** | Mast, boom or yard; any pole used in the rigging. |
| **Starting** | Strike at random with cane or knotted cord. |
| **Stanchion** | Upright bar or beam used as support. |
| **Stem** | Forepart of ship. |
| **Stern** | Aftpart of ship. |
| **Storm jib** | Small triangular sail in the bow of a vessel. |
| **Sunwise** | Or deiseil; a right-hand turn or circle, used since Celtic times to bring good luck. |
| **Tack** | Course of a ship in relation to the position of her sails; to shift course by altering the sails. |
| **Taffrail** | Rail round the stern of ship. |
| **Topmast** | Masts were/are made of three spars ; lower, top, topgallant. |
| **Topsail schooner** | A schooner with square topsails above her fore and aft sails. |
| **Tweendecks** | Between decks. |
| **Waist** | The part of a ship between the forecastle and quarterdeck. Also called the spar-deck as spare spars were stowed here. |
| **Windward** | Toward the wind |
| **Yard** | Spar to which a square sail is secured at its head |
| **Zuider Zee** | Former gulf of the North Sea. Reclaimed this century and now part of the Netherlands. |

# Bibliography

Barraclough, Geoffrey (ed.) *The Times Atlas of World History*. BCA, 1994.
Barrow, G.W.S. *Robert Bruce*. Edinburgh University Press, 1976.
Baynham, Henry *Before the Mast*. Arrow Books, 1972.
Beckett, Derrick *Brunel's Britain*. David and Charles, 1980.
Berlitz, Charles *The Bermuda Triangle*. Souvenir Press, 1974.
Black, Clinton, V. *The Story of Jamaica*. Collins, 1965.
Bradford, Ernle *The Sultan's Admiral*. Hodder and Stoughton, 1969.
Braynard, Frank O. and Miller, William H. *Fifty Famous Ocean Liners*. Patrick Stephens, 1982.
Breed, Bryan *Famous Mysteries of the Sea*. Arthur Barker, 1965.
Brewer, Ebenezer Cobham (rev. Evans, Ivor) *Wordsworth Dictionary of Phrase and Fable*. Cassell & Co., 1970.
Carpenter, Rhys *Beyond the Pillars of Hercules*. Tandem, 1973.
Castlereagh, Duncan *The Great Age of Exploration*. Reader's Digest Assoc., 1971.
Chichester, Francis *Along the Clipper Way*. Hodder and Stoughton, 1966.
Clark, A.H. *The Clipper Ship Era*. Putnam & Sons, 1970.
Clowes, G.S. Laird, *The Story of Sail*. Eyre & Spottiswood, 1936.
Dillon, Mykes & Chadwick, Nora *The Celtic Realms*. Cardinal/Sphere, 1973.
Du Baty, Capt Raymond *15,000 Miles in a Ketch*. Nelson & Sons, 1942.
Edey, Maitland, A. *The Sea Traders*. Time Life Books, 1971.
Eunson, Jerry *The Shipwrecks of Fair Isle*. W.S.Wilson, 1963.
Fairley, John & Welfare, Simon *Arthur C. Clarke's Chronicle of the Strange and Mysterious*. BCA, 1987.
Falkus, Hugh *Master of Cape Horn*. Victor Gollancz, 1982.
Ferguson, David *Shipwrecks of North East Scotland 1444-1990*. Aberdeen University Press, 1991.
Francis, Daniel *Arctic Chase*. Topsail Books, 1984.
Fraser, Duncan *The Smugglers*. Standard Press, 1971.
Frazer, James *The Golden Bough*. Macmillan, 1990.
Grimal, Pierre (ed.) *World Mythology*. Larousse/Hamlyn, 1965.
Harris, John *Without Trace*. Methuen, 1981.
Hartman, Tom *Guinness Book of Ships and Shipping*. Guinness Superlatives, 1983.
Haythornthwaite, Philip *Nelson's Navy*. Osprey, 1993.

Jackson, Gordon *The British Whaling Trade*. Adam and Charles Black, 1978
Jackson, John.J. *Bermuda*. David and Charles, 1988.
Jones , Alison *Larousse Dictionary of World Folklore*. Larousse, 1995.
Keating, Laurence *The Great Mary Celeste Hoax*. Heath Cranston, 1921.
Kusche, Lawrence *The Bermuda Triangle Mystery – Solved*. New English Library, 1975.
Lawrie, Alastair, Matthews, Hellen & Ritchie, Douglas (eds.) *Glimmer of Cold Brine*. Aberdeen University Press, 1988.
Leach, Maria (ed.) *Funk and Wagnalls Standard Dictionary of Folklore, Mythology And Legend*. NEL, 1972.
Lubbock, Basil *China Clippers*. Brown, Son and Ferguson, 1914.
Lubbock, Basil *Last of the Windjammers Vol 1*. Brown, Son and Ferguson, 1927.
Lubbock, Basil *Last of the Windjammers Vol 2*. Brown, Son and Ferguson, 1929.
Lubbock, Basil *The Colonial Clippers*. Brown Son and Ferguson, 1924.
Lubbock, Basil *The Arctic Whalers*. Brown, Son and Ferguson, 1955.
Lucie-Smith, Edward *Outcasts of the Sea*. Paddington Press, 1978.
McEvedy, Colin *The Penguin Atlas of Ancient History*. Penguin, 1967.
McEvedy, Colin *The Penguin Atlas of Mediaeval History*. Penguin, 1961.
McEvedy, Colin *The Penguin Atlas of Modern History*. Penguin, 1972.
McGowran, Tom *Newhaven-on-Forth*. John Donald, 1985.
Mackintosh, W.R. *Around the Orkney Peat Fires*. Kirkwall Press, 1967.
Maclean, Alastair *Captain Cook*. Collins, 1972.
MacNeill, F. Marian *The Silver Bough*. Canongate Classics, 1989.
Matthews, John and Caitlin *British and Irish Mythology*. Diamond Books, 1995.
Neatby, Leslie *Search for Franklin*. Hurtig Publishing, 1970.
Owen, Roderick *The Fate of Franklin*. Hutchinson, 1978.
Pack, Capt. J. OBE RN *Nelson's Blood (The story of naval rum)*. Alan Sutton, 1995.
Parkinson, C. Northcote *Britannia Rules*. Alan Sutton Publishing, 1983.
Runciman, Walter *Before the Mast and After*. T Fisher Unwin, 1924.
Smeeton, Miles '*...because the Horn is there...*' Nautical Publishing, 1970.
Smyth, Alfred P. *Warlords and Holy Men*. Edinburgh University Press, 1989.
Stammers, Michael *The Passage Makers*. Teredo Books, 1978.
Still, W. N. (ed.) *The Confederate Navy*. Conway Maritime Press, 1971.
Stevenson, John *Popular Disturbances in England 1700 – 1832*. Longman, 1992.
Thomson, George Malcolm *Sir Francis Drake*. BCA, 1972.
Thomson, George Malcolm *The North West Passage*. Futura, 1975.
Varende, Jean de la *Cherish the Sea*. Sidgwick and Jackson, 1955.
Villiers, Alan *The Last of the Wind Ships*. J. Routledge & Son, 1934.
Villiers, Alan *The War with Cape Horn*. Hodder and Stoughton, 1971.
Ward, M. *The Blessed Trade*. Michael Joseph, 1971.
Warren, Mark D. (ed.) *Ocean Liners of the Past - Lusitania*. Patrick Stephens, 1970.
Warren, Mark D. (ed.) *Ocean Liners of the Past - Mauritania*. Patrick Stephens, 1970.
Wellesley, Kenneth (trans.) *Tacitus, The Histories*. The Penguin Classics, 1964.
Whipple, A.B.C. *Tall Ships and Great Captains*. Gollancz,1961.
Winston, Alexander *Pirates and Privateers*. Arrow, 1972.

## OTHERS – NOT IN BOOK FORM

Eileen Edwards, Merseyside Maritime Museum.
The late Mr Douglas Doyle of Natal, South Africa.
The late Thomas R. Archibald, ex-Ben Line.
*Edinburgh Evening News*.
*Dundee Courier*.
*London Times*.